*New Accents*

General Editor: TERENCE HAWKES

# FANTASY:
## THE LITERATURE OF SUBVERSION

ROSEMARY JACKSON

# FANTASY:
## THE LITERATURE OF SUBVERSION

LONDON AND NEW YORK

1117772

*First published in 1981 by*
*Methuen & Co. Ltd*
*Reprinted twice*
*Reprinted 1986*

*Reprinted 1988, 1991, 1993, 1995*
*by Routledge*
*11 New Fetter Lane, London EC4P 4EE*
*29 West 35th Street, New York, NY 10001*

*Printed in Great Britain by*
*J.W. Arrowsmith Ltd, Bristol*

British Library Cataloging in Publication Data

*Jackson, Rosemary*
　　*Fantasy, the literature of subversion. – (New accents).*
　　*1. Fantastic fiction, European – History and criticism*
　　*2. European fiction – 18th century – History and criticism*
　　*3. European fiction – 19th century – History and criticism*
　　*4. European fiction – 20th century – History and criticism*
　　*I. Title      II. Series*
　　*809.3'9'15      PN3435      80-41387*

*ISBN 0-415-02562-1*

# CONTENTS

# GENERAL EDITOR'S PREFACE

How can we recognise or deal with the new? Any equipment we bring to the task will have been designed to engage with the old: it will look for and identify extensions and developments of what we already know. To some degree the unprecedented will always be unthinkable.

The *New Accents* series has made its own wary negotiation around that paradox, turning it, over the years, into the central concern of a continuing project. We are obliged, of course, to be bold. Change is our proclaimed business, innovation our announced quarry, the accents of the future the language in which we deal. So we have sought, and still seek, to confront and respond to those developments in literary studies that seem crucial aspects of the tidal waves of transformation that continue to sweep across our culture. Areas such as structuralism, post-structuralism, feminism, marxism, semiotics, subculture, deconstruction, dialogism, post-modernism, and the new attention to the nature and modes of language, politics and way of life that these bring, have already been the primary concern of a large number of our volumes. Their 'nuts and bolts' exposition of the issues at stake in new ways of writing texts and new ways of reading them has proved an effective stratagem against perplexity.

But the question of what 'texts' are or may be has also become more and more complex. It is not just the impact of electronic modes of communication, such as computer networks and data banks, that has forced us to revise our sense of the sort of material to which the process called 'reading' may apply. Satellite television and supersonic travel have eroded the traditional capacities of time and space to confirm prejudice, reinforce ignorance, and conceal significant difference. Ways of life and cultural practices of which we had barely heard can now be set compellingly beside – can even confront – our own. The effect is to make us ponder the culture we have inherited; to see it, perhaps for the first time, as an intricate, continuing construction. And that means that we can also begin to see, and to question, those arrangements of foregrounding and backgrounding, of stressing and repressing, of placing at the centre and of restricting to the periphery, that give our own way of life its distinctive character.

Small wonder if, nowadays, we frequently find ourselves at the boundaries of the precedented and at the limit of the thinkable: peering into an abyss out of which there begin to lurch awkwardly-formed monsters with unaccountable – yet unavoidable – demands on our attention. These may involve unnerving styles of narrative, unsettling notions of 'history', unphilosophical ideas about 'philosophy', even un-childish views of 'comics', to say nothing of a host of barely respectable activities for which we have no reassuring names.

In this situation, straightforward elucidation, careful unpicking, informative bibliographies, can offer positive help, and each *New Accents* volume will continue to include these. But if the project of closely scrutinising the new remains nonetheless a disconcerting one, there are still overwhelming reasons for giving it all the consideration we can muster. The unthinkable, after all, is that which covertly shapes our thoughts.

TERENCE HAWKES

# ACKNOWLEDGEMENTS

I WOULD like to thank many friends and colleagues for their encouragement whilst I was writing this book. I am particularly grateful to Dr Linda Gillman, who was immensely generous with her ideas, criticism and love, and to Dr Allon White, who offered invaluable intellectual help. Thanks to students and lecturers in the School of English and American Studies, University of East Anglia, especially to Jon Cook, David Punter, Don Ranvaud and Dr Allan Smith. Also many thanks to Gay Clifford, Ann Cook, Michael DaCosta, Gérard van Eyk, Dr Penny Florence, Barbara Lloyd, Mary Smart, Geoffrey Summerfield, Nicole Ward-Jouve. And to my son, Adam.

ROSEMARY JACKSON
UNIVERSITY OF EAST ANGLIA, 1980

**Note**

Editions of primary literary texts are identified in the notes which are printed, by chapter, before the bibliography. All secondary works (including those mentioned in the notes) are listed in the bibliography, in alphabetical order under the name of the author.

Only the perverse fantasy can still save us.

Goethe

Literature of the fantastic is concerned to describe desire in its excessive forms as well as in its various transformations or perversions.

Todorov

When our eye sees a monstrous deed, our soul stands still.

Fassbinder

The only thing you can do if you are trapped in a reflection is to invert the image.

Juliet Mitchell

# 1 INTRODUCTION

> Human nature, essentially changeable, unstable as the dust, can endure no restraint; if it binds itself it soon begins to tear madly at its bonds, until it rends everything asunder, the wall, the bonds and its very self ... My inquiry is purely historical; no lightning flashes any longer from the long since vanished thunder-clouds. ... The limits which my capacity for thought imposes upon me are narrow enough, but the province to be traversed here is infinite.
>
> Franz Kafka, *The Great Wall of China*[1]

FANTASY, both in literature and out of it, is an enormous and seductive subject. Its association with imagination and with desire has made it an area difficult to articulate or to define, and indeed the 'value' of fantasy has seemed to reside in precisely this resistance to definition, in its 'free-floating' and escapist qualities. Literary fantasies have appeared to be 'free' from many of the conventions and restraints of more realistic texts: they have refused to observe unities of time, space and character, doing away with chronology, three-dimensionality and with rigid distinctions between animate and inanimate objects, self and other, life and death. Given this resistance of fantasy to narrow categorization and definition, it might seem self-defeating to attempt to produce a critical study which proposes to 'schematize' or 'theorize' about fantasy in literature and thereby to militate against escapism or a simple pleasure principle. Since this book does attempt such a study, it is best, perhaps, to try to clarify at the outset some of the theoretical and critical assumptions upon which it is based.

English literary criticism has been notoriously untheoretical in its approach to works of fantasy, as to other texts. Despite the growth of interdisciplinary studies in British institutions during the last decade, the impact of Marxist, linguistic and psychoanalytic theory upon readings of literature has been safely buffered by a solid tradition of liberal humanism, nowhere more so than in readings of fantasy, where a transcendentalist criticism has seemed to be justified. Literature of the fantastic has been claimed as 'transcending' reality, 'escaping' the human condition and constructing superior alternate, 'secondary' worlds. From W.H. Auden, C.S. Lewis and J.R.R. Tolkien, this notion of fantasy literature as fulfilling a desire for a 'better', more complete, unified reality has come to dominate readings of the fantastic, defining it as an art form providing vicarious gratification. This book aims to locate such a transcendentalist approach as part of a nostalgic, humanistic vision, of the same kind as those romance fictions produced by Lewis, Tolkien, T.H. White and other modern fabulists, all of whom look back to a lost moral and social hierarchy, which their fantasies attempt to recapture and revivify.

Particularly pertinent to an argument against transcendentalist fiction and criticism is a famous passage from *The German Ideology*, in which Marx and Engels urge the importance of situating art within the historical and cultural framework from which it is produced. They write:

> In direct contrast to German philosophy which descends from heaven to earth, here we ascend from earth to

heaven. . . . The phantoms formed in the human brain are also, necessarily, sublimates of their [men's] material life process, which is empirically verifiable and bound to material premises. (p.47)

Like any other text, a literary fantasy is produced within, and determined by, its social context. Though it might struggle against the limits of this context, often being articulated upon that very struggle, it cannot be understood in isolation from it. The forms taken by any particular fantastic text are determined by a number of forces which intersect and interact in different ways in each individual work. Recognition of these forces involves placing authors in relation to historical, social, economic, political and sexual determinants, as well as to a literary tradition of fantasy, and makes it impossible to accept a reading of this kind of literature which places it somehow mysteriously 'outside' time altogether. In a book of this length, it is impossible to consider all, or many, of these determinants in connection with every text, but my approach throughout is founded on the assumption that the literary fantastic is never 'free'. Although surviving as a perennial mode and present in works by authors as different as Petronius, Poe and Pynchon, the fantastic is transformed according to these authors' diverse historical positions. A more extensive treatment would relate texts more specifically to the conditions of their production, to the particular constraints against which the fantasy protests and from which it is generated, for fantasy characteristically attempts to compensate for a lack resulting from cultural constraints: it is a literature of desire, which seeks that which is experienced as absence and loss.

In expressing desire, fantasy can operate in two ways (according to the different meanings of 'express'): it can *tell of*, manifest or show desire (expression in the sense of portrayal, representation, manifestation, linguistic utterance, mention, description), or it can *expel* desire, when this desire is a disturbing element which threatens cultural order and continuity (expression in the sense of pressing out, squeezing, expulsion, getting rid of something by force). In many cases fantastic literature fulfils both functions at once, for desire can be 'expelled' through having been 'told of' and thus vicariously experienced by author and reader. In this way fantastic literature points to or suggests the basis upon which cultural order rests, for it opens up, for a brief moment, on to disorder, on to illegality, on to that which lies outside the law, that which is outside dominant value systems. The fantastic traces the unsaid and the unseen of culture: that which has been silenced, made invisible, covered over and made 'absent'. The movement from the first to the second of these functions, from expression as manifestation to expression as expulsion, is one of the recurrent features of fantastic narrative, as it tells of the impossible attempt to realize desire, to make visible the invisible and to discover absence. Telling implies using the language of the dominant order and so accepting its norms, re-covering its dark areas. Since this excursion into disorder can only begin from a base within the dominant cultural order, literary fantasy is a telling index of the limits of that order. Its introduction of the 'unreal' is set against the category of the 'real' – a category which the fantastic interrogates by its difference.

As a literature of 'unreality', fantasy has altered in character over the years in accordance with changing notions of what exactly constitutes 'reality'. Modern fantasy is rooted in ancient myth, mysticism, folklore, fairy tale and romance. The most obvious starting point for this study was the late eighteenth century – the point at which industrialization transformed western society. From about 1800 onwards, those fantasies produced within a capitalist economy express some of the debilitating psychological effects of inhabiting a materialistic culture. They are peculiarly violent and horrific.

This book concentrates upon literary fantasies of the last two centuries, fantasies produced within a post-Romantic, secularized culture. One purpose of drawing together a number of different texts of this period was to see what features, if any, they had in common, and what conclusions might be drawn from their possible identification. It was in the course of reading and comparing a wide variety of fiction, from Gothic novels, through Dickens and Victorian fantasists, to Dostoevsky, Kafka, Peake and Pynchon, that a pattern began to emerge for me, a pattern which suggested that similarities on levels of theme and structure were more than coincidental.

The most important and influential critical study of fantasy of this post-Romantic period is Tzvetan Todorov's *The Fantastic: A Structural Approach to a Literary Genre* (1973). The value of Todorov's work in encouraging serious critical engagement with a form of literature which had been dismissed as being rather frivolous or foolish cannot be over-estimated, and anyone working in this area has to acknowledge a large debt to his study.

Previous French critics, such as P.-G. Castex, Marcel Schneider, Louis Vax and Roger Caillois, had tried to define literary fantasy by cataloguing its recurrent themes and motifs, taken rather randomly from various works. Schneider had claimed the fantastic as dramatizing 'the anxiety of existence', whilst Caillois described it as a form which was stranded between a serene mysticism and a purely humanistic psychology. Todorov has little time for metaphysics and he opposes impressionistic attempts to define fantasy. He is not interested in the semantic approach of many other critics (looking for clusters of subjects and for the meaning of the fantastic in these subjects), and he turns instead to a structural analysis of fantastic literature, seeking structural features which different texts have in common and which might provide a more concrete definition of the fantastic.

Nevertheless, there are some important omissions in Todorov's book, and it was in an attempt to go some way towards filling these that the present work was begun. For, in common with much structuralist criticism, Todorov's *The Fantastic* fails to consider the social and political implications of literary forms. Its attention is confined to the effects of the text and the means of its operation. It does not move outwards again to relate the forms of literary texts to their cultural formation. It is in an attempt to suggest ways of remedying this that my study tries to extend Todorov's investigation from being one limited to the *poetics* of the fantastic into one aware of the *politics* of its forms.

Fantasy in literature deals so blatantly and repeatedly with unconscious material that it seems rather absurd to try to understand its significance without some reference to psychoanalysis and psychoanalytic readings of texts. Yet Todorov repudiates Freudian theory as inadequate or irrelevant when approaching the fantastic. I take this to be the major blind-spot of his book and one which is bound up with his neglect of political or ideological issues. For it is in the unconscious that social structures and 'norms' are reproduced and sustained within us, and only by redirecting attention to this area can we begin to perceive the ways in which the relations between society and the individual are fixed. As Juliet Mitchell writes,

> The way we live as 'ideas' the necessary laws of human society is not so much conscious as *unconscious* – the particular task of psychoanalysis is to decipher how we acquire our heritage of the ideas and laws of human society within the unconscious mind, or, to put it another way, the unconscious mind *is* the way in which we acquire these laws.[2]

Psychoanalysis directs itself towards an unravelling of these laws, trying to comprehend how social structures are represented and sustained within and through us in our unconscious. Literary fantasies, expressing unconscious drives, are particularly open to psychoanalytic readings, and frequently show in graphic forms a tension between the 'laws of human society' and the resistance of the unconscious mind to those laws. I shall discuss some of these features in the chapter on fantasy and psychoanalysis, returning to the work of Freud and referring to the writings of Jacques Lacan as providing a theoretical base in approaching the relation between ideology and unconscious life. In many ways this chapter provides the centre of my arguments and is the most crucial in trying to stretch Todorov's ideas into a more widely based cultural study of the fantastic.

This study is divided into two sections. The first section is theoretical, examining the conditions and the possibilities of fantasy as a literary mode in terms of its forms, features, basic elements and structures. The term 'mode' is being employed here to identify structural features underlying various works in different periods of time.

> For when we speak of a mode, what can we mean but that this particular type of literary discourse is not bound to the conventions of a given age, nor indissolubly linked to a given type of verbal artifact, but rather persists as a temptation and a mode of expression across a whole range of historical periods, seeming to offer itself, if only intermittently, as a formal possibility which can be revived and renewed.[3]

It could be suggested that fantasy is a literary mode from which a number of related genres emerge. Fantasy provides a range of possibilities out of which various combinations produce different kinds of fiction in different historical situations. Borrowing linguistic terms, the basic model of fantasy could be seen as a language, or *langue*, from which its various forms, or *paroles*, derive. Out of this mode develops romance literature or 'the marvellous' (including fairy tales and science fiction), 'fantastic' literature (including stories by Poe, Isak Dinesen, Maupassant, Gautier, Kafka, H.P. Lovecraft) and related tales of abnormal psychic states, delusion, hallucination, etc.

This is not to imply that an ideal theoretical model exists to which all fantasies should conform. There is no abstract entity called 'fantasy'; there is only a range of different works which have similar structural characteristics and which seem to be generated by similar unconscious desires. Through their particular manifestations of desire, they can be associated together. The possibilities available to each particular text are determined, in many ways, by the texts which have preceded it and whose characteristic features it repeats or repudiates. Like dreams, with which they have many similarities, literary fantasies are made up of many elements re-combined, and are inevitably determined by the range of those constitutive elements available to the author/dreamer. Freud writes, 'The "creative" imagination, indeed, is quite incapable of *inventing* anything; it can only combine components that are strange to one another.'[4] Again, 'In the psychic life, there is nothing arbitrary, nothing undetermined.' [5] Fantasy is not to do with inventing another non-human world: it is not transcendental. It has to do with inverting elements of this world, re-combining its constitutive features in new relations to produce something strange, unfamiliar and *apparently* 'new', absolutely 'other' and different.

The theoretical section, then, introduces critical material on literary fantasy, both from a structuralist position, looking at the *narrative qualities* of the mode, and from a psychoanalytical perspective, considering these features as the *narrative effects* of basic psychic impulses.

The second section of the book looks at a number of texts in a little more detail. It does not attempt a comprehensive 'survey' of post-Romantic fantasy, but it does include a wide variety of diverse works to give a sense of the striking recurrence and similarity of several thematic and formal clusters. It thus reinforces the argument against any particular fantasy's 'difference' or 'peculiarity'. Detailed exposition has, unfortunately, had to be sacrificed. As to the selection of texts, there is reference to French, German, Russian and American literature, but the bias is quantitatively towards English works, for reasons of familiarity and convenience.

Texts which receive most attention are those which reveal most clearly some of the points raised in the theoretical section – not in order to prove a hypothetical argument, but because it is in these works that the subversive function of the fantastic is most apparent. Although nearly all literary fantasies eventually re-cover desire, neutralizing their own impulses towards transgression, some move towards the extreme position which will be found in Sade's writings, and attempt to remain 'open', dissatisfied, endlessly desiring. Those texts which attempt that movement and that transgressive function have been given most space in this book, for in them the fantastic is at its most uncompromising in its interrogation of the 'nature' of the 'real'.

One consequence of this focus is that some of the better known authors of fantasy works (in the popular sense) are given less space than might be expected. For example, the best-selling fantasies by Kingsley, Lewis, Tolkien, Le Guin or Richard Adams are not discussed at great length. This is not simply through prejudice against their particular ideals, nor through an attempt to recommend other texts as more 'progressive' in any easy way, but because they belong to that realm of fantasy which is more properly defined as faery, or romance literature. The moral and religious allegories, parables and fables informing the stories of Kingsley and Tolkien move away from the unsettling implications which are found at the centre of the purely 'fantastic'. Their original impulse may be similar, but they move from it, expelling their desire and frequently displacing it into religious longing and nostalgia. Thus they defuse potentially disturbing, anti-social drives and retreat from any profound confrontation with existential dis-ease. Writers whose discontent is less easily repressed are given correspondingly more attention, not least because of the relative critical neglect they have suffered to date – hardly surprising in terms of the close relation that has existed between literary criticism and a body of literature which supports orthodox behaviour and conservative institutions. By the same criterion, some novelists who are not normally thought of as working within a fantastic mode are included because of the way in which elements of fantasy enter into, disrupt and disturb the body of their texts. So alongside Mary Shelley, James Hogg, Edgar Allan Poe, R.L. Stevenson and Kafka lie George Eliot, Joseph Conrad and Henry James, as well as 'fantastic realists' such as Dickens and Dostoevsky.

All of this leaves aside the pleasures (of various kinds) of reading literary fantasy. This is really another area for psychoanalysis. I can only say that I have no desire to deprive the reader of the pleasure of the text. The reluctance to let works rest as closed or 'innocent' or pleasure-giving objects derives from a need to understand what might be going on under the cover of this pleasure. De-mystifying the process of reading fantasies will, hopefully, point to the possibility of undoing many texts which work, unconsciously, upon us. In the end this may lead to real social transformation.

# PART ONE: THEORY

# 2 THE FANTASTIC AS A MODE

## The imagination in exile

> There would be tears and there would be strange laughter. Fierce births and deaths beneath umbrageous ceilings. And dreams, and violence, and disenchantment.
> Mervyn Peake, *Titus Groan*

THE 'FANTASTIC' derives from the Latin, *phantasticus*, which is from the Greek φαντάζω, meaning to make visible or manifest. In this general sense, all imaginary activity is fantastic, all literary works are fantasies. Given such and infinite scope, it has proved difficult to develop an adequate definition of fantasy as a literary kind. One critic claims that 'in no significant senses does fantasy have a history' (Irwin, p.x). It seems appropriate that such a protean form has so successfully resisted generic classification. 'The wide range of works which we call . . . fantastic is large, much too large to constitute a single genre. [It includes] whole conventional genres, such as fairy tale, detective story, Fantasy' (Rabkin, p.118).

As a critical term, 'fantasy' has been applied rather indiscriminately to any literature which does not give priority to realistic representation: myths, legends, folk and fairy tales, utopian allegories, dream visions, surrealist texts, science fiction, horror stories, all presenting realms 'other' than the human. A characteristic most frequently associated with literary fantasy has been its obdurate refusal of prevailing definitions of the 'real' or 'possible', a refusal amounting at times to violent opposition. 'A fantasy is a story based on and controlled by an overt violation of what is generally accepted as possibility; it is the narrative result of transforming the condition contrary to fact into "fact" itself' (Irwin, p.x). Such violation of dominant assumptions threatens to subvert (overturn, upset, undermine) rules and conventions taken to be normative. This is not in itself a socially subversive activity: it would be naive to equate fantasy with either anarchic or revolutionary politics. It does, however, disturb 'rules' of artistic representation and literature's reproduction of the 'real'.

An examination of some of the roots of literary fantasy reveals it to be characterized by this subversive function. Mikhail Bakhtin's study, *Problems of Dostoevsky's Poetics*, places modern fantasists such as E.T.A. Hoffmann, Dostoevsky, Gogol, Edgar Allan Poe, Jean-Paul, as the direct descendants of a traditional literary genre: the *menippea*. Menippean satire was present in ancient Christian and Byzantine literature, in medieval, Renaissance, and Reformation writings. Its most representative works were fictions such as Petronius's *Satyricon*, Varro's *Bimarcus* (i.e. *The Double Marcus*), Apuleius's *Metamorphoses* (known as *The Golden Ass*), Lucian's *Strange Story*. It was a genre which broke the demands of historical realism or probability. The *menippea* moved easily in space between this world, an underworld and an upper world. It conflated past, present and future, and allowed dialogues with the dead. States of hallucination, dream, insanity, eccentric behaviour and speech, personal transformation, extraordinary situations, were the norm.

> Characteristic of the menippea are violations of the generally accepted, ordinary course of events and of the established norms of behaviour and etiquette, including

the verbal. . . . Scandals and eccentricities destroy the epical and tragical integrity of the world, they form a breach in the stable, normal course of human affairs and events and free human behaviour from predetermining norms and motivations. (Bakhtin, p.96)

It was a genre which did not claim to be definitive or knowing. Lacking finality, it interrogated authoritative truths and replaced them with something less certain. As Bakhtin puts it, 'The fantastic serves here not in the positive *embodiment* of the truth, but in the search after the truth, its provocation and, most importantly, its *testing*' (p.94).

Bakhtin's generic definitions of the *menippea* and his discovery of similar features in the works of Rabelais, Swift, Sterne, Dickens, Dostoevsky, Gogol, are useful as an introduction to the qualities and functions of fantastic texts. He points towards fantasy's hostility to static, discrete units, to its juxtaposition of incompatible elements and its resistance to fixity. Spatial, temporal, and philosophical ordering systems all dissolve; unified notions of character are broken; language and syntax become incoherent. Through its 'misrule', it permits 'ultimate questions' about social order, or metaphysical riddles as to life's purpose. Unable to give affirmation to a closed, unified, or omniscient vision, the *menippea* violates social propriety. It tells of descents into underworlds of brothels, prisons, orgies, graves: it has no fear of the criminal, erotic, mad, or dead. Many modern fantasies continue this violently transgressive function, but there are crucial differences between the delight in misrule found in a menippean tradition and the less sanguine, less celebratory disorders found in Dostoevsky and later fantasists, differences which Bakhtin tends to minimize.

For Bakhtin, the *menippea* was conceptually linked with the notion of carnival; carnival was a public activity, a ritualized, festive event. 'In the carnival', continues Bakhtin, 'everyone is an active participant, everyone communes in the carnival act . . . The carnival life is life drawn out of its usual rut, it is to a degree "life turned inside out", "life the wrong way round" ' (p.101). Carnival was a temporary condition, a ritualized suspension of everyday law and order. By those means carnival dissolved differences, permitted free contact between various ranks, broke sexual taboos and merged together 'all the things that were closed off, isolated and separated in carnivalistic contacts and combinations' (p.101).

The *menippea* was a traditional form of fantastic art, and it exhibits crucial links with carnival as well as crucial differences between its celebration of misrule and the disorder found in less festive modern fantasies. Dostoevsky's tales, for example, *Bobok, The Double, The Underground Man, A Nasty Story, The Dream of a Queer Fellow*, retain many carnivalesque features. They invert rules, introduce the unexpected, tell of 'abnormal' psychological states, descend into a social underworld. But they have no communal base. Far from celebrating a temporary suspense of the law, they exist outside it. Their hallucinating subjects are isolated from a community, believing their estrangement to be peculiar to themselves. They are eccentric (ex-centric), have ceased to 'coincide with themselves' (Bakhtin's phrase), and experience themselves as double, often multiple, identities. This disintegration of personal unity is rather different from the temporary suspensions of coherence in the traditional *menippea*.

Modern fantasy is severed from its roots in carnivalesque art: it is no longer a communal form. The disunities found in Dostoevsky, Poe, Kafka or Pynchon are not the temporary ones of menippean misrule, although their grotesque manifestations are similar. Bakhtin suggests that the 'polyphonic' novel of Dostoevsky expresses a mixing together of heterogeneous social forms as one of the consequences of capitalist economy and its destruction of 'organic' order. 'Capitalism, leaving no other divisions but the division into proletarians and capitalists, caused those worlds to collide and welded them together in its own contradictory, evolving unity' (p.15). The fantastic texts of Dostoevsky anticipate one of the central features of modern literature: a plurality of languages, a confrontation of discourse and ideology, without any definitive conclusion or synthesis – there is no 'monologism', no 'axis'.[1] There is only a grotesque dissolution, a promiscuity.

Dostoevsky frequently writes of a fantastic literature as being the only appropriate medium for suggesting a sense of estrangement, of alienation from 'natural' origins. His fictions narrate metropolitan scenes which are 'un-natural', inhabited by disintegrated subjects, 'underground men'. Although the fantastic retains its original function of exerting pressure against dominant hierarchical systems, it is no longer an escapist form, but the only expressive mode. As Dostoevsky writes,

> But now you know that if there is no soil and if there is no action possible, the striving spirit will precisely express itself in abnormal and irregular manifestations – it will mistake the phrase for life, it will pounce upon the ready but alien formula, it will be only too glad to have it, and will substitute it for reality! In a fantastic life all functions, too, are fantastic. (Dostoevsky, cit. Linnér, p.55)

Sartre has written a defence of fantasy as a perennial form coming into its own in the secularized, materialistic world of modern capitalism. Whilst religious faith prevailed, writes Sartre, fantasy told of leaps into other realms. Through asceticism, mysticism, metaphysics, or poetry, the conditions of a purely human existence were transcended, and fantasy fulfilled a definite, escapist, function. 'It manifested our human power to transcend the human. Men strove to create a world that was not of this world' (Sartre, 1947, p.58). In a secular culture, fantasy has a different function. It does not invent supernatural regions, but presents a natural world inverted into something strange, something 'other'. It becomes 'domesticated', humanized, turning from transcendental explorations to transcriptions of a human condition. In this sense, Sartre claims, fantasy assumes its proper function: to transform this world. '*The fantastic, in becoming humanized, approaches the ideal purity of its essence, becomes what it had been*.' Without a context of faith in supernaturalism (whether sacred or secular), fantasy is an expression of human forces.

> It seems to be stripped of all its artifices. . . . We recognize the footprint on the shore as our own. There are no phantoms, no succubi, no weeping fountains. There are only men, and the creator of the fantastic announces that he identifies himself with the fantastic object. (pp. 59–60)

Sartre defines the fantastic as a literature in which definitive meanings are unknown: objects no longer serve transcendent purposes, so that means have replaced ends.

There was no facile transition from faith to disbelief: transformations of fantasy were slow and fluid and the survival of the 'marvellous' in twentieth-century works indicates that mode's continuing seductiveness. But the fantastic has become a narrative form which is peculiarly disenchanted (in both senses of the word). 'The period of unbelief allowed for the emergence of fantastic literature in its strictest sense.' [2] 'The fantastic is a compensation that man provides for himself, at the level of imagination [l'imaginaire], for what he has lost at the level of faith' (Lévy, p.617).

Georges Bataille writes, 'Those arts which sustain anguish and the recovery from anguish within us, are the heirs of religion' (Bataille, *Literature and Evil*, p.16). Fantasy betrays a dissatisfaction with what 'is', but its frustrated attempts to realize an ideal make it a negative version of religious myth. Fantasy is 'sovereign (only) in the desire for the object, not the possession of it' (ibid.). Without a cosmology of heaven and hell, the mind faces mere redundancy: the cosmos becomes a space full of menace, increasingly apprehended and internalized as an area of non-meaning.

## The 'real' under scrutiny

> Reality is not limited to the familiar, the commonplace,
> for it consists in huge part of a *latent, as yet unspoken future
> word*.
>
> <div align="right">Dostoevsky, <i>Notebooks</i></div>

In a secularized culture, desire for otherness is not displaced
into alternative regions of heaven or hell, but is directed
towards the absent areas of this world, transforming it into
something 'other' than the familiar, comfortable one.
Instead of an alternative order, it creates 'alterity', this world
re-placed and dis-located. A useful term for understanding
and expressing this process of transformation and deformation is 'paraxis'. This signifies par-axis, that which lies
on either side of the principle axis, that which lies alongside
the main body. Paraxis is a telling notion in relation to the
place, or space, of the fantastic, for it implies an inextricable
link to the main body of the 'real' which it shades and
threatens.

The term paraxis is also a technical one employed in
optics. A paraxial region is an area in which light rays *seem* to
unite at a point after refraction. In this area, object and
image seem to collide, but in fact neither object nor reconsti-
tuted image genuinely reside there: nothing does.

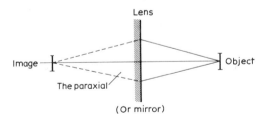

This paraxial area could be taken to represent the spectral
region of the fantastic, whose imaginary world is neither
entirely 'real' (object), nor entirely 'unreal' (image), but is
located somewhere indeterminately between the two. This

paraxial positioning determines many of the structural and semantic features of fantastic narrative: its means of establishing its 'reality' are initially mimetic ('realistic', presenting an 'object' world 'objectively') but then move into another mode which would seem to be marvellous ('unrealistic', representing apparent impossibilities), were it not for its initial grounding in the 'real'. Thematically too, as we shall see, the fantastic plays upon difficulties of interpreting events/things as objects or as images, thus disorientating the reader's categorization of the 'real'.

The etymology of the word 'fantastic' points to an essential ambiguity: it is *un*-real. Like the ghost which is neither dead nor alive, the fantastic is a spectral presence, suspended between being and nothingness. It takes the real and breaks it. Coleridge's famous distinction between Imagination and Fancy (employed interchangeably with Fantasy) in his *Biographia Literaria*, emphasizes this dissolving activity, this re-creating of the real: 'Fancy has no other counters to play with but fixities and definites . . . It is a mode of memory emancipated from the order of time and place, blended with and modified by that empirical phenomenon of the will, which we express by the word *choice*' (p.167). J.A. Symonds writes similarly, linking it to the grotesque: 'The fantastic . . . invariably implies a certain exaggeration or distortion of nature. What we call fantastic in art results from an exercise of the capricious fancy, playing with things which it combines into arbitrary, nonexistent forms.' Fantasy re-combines and inverts the real, but it does not escape it: it exists in a parasitical or symbiotic relation to the real. The fantastic cannot exist independently of that 'real' world which it seems to find so frustratingly finite.

The best theoretical study of fantasy as a mode defined by its 'relationality', i.e. by its positioning in relation to the real, is Irène Bessière's *Le récit fantastique: la poètique de l'incertain* (1974). The fantastic is seen by Bessière as intimately linked to the real and rational: it is not to be equated with irrationality. Anti-rational, it is the inverse side of reason's orthodoxy. It reveals reason and reality to be arbitrary, shifting constructs, and thereby scrutinizes the category of the 'real'. Contradictions surface and are held antinomically in the fantastic text, as reason is made to confront all that it traditionally refuses to encounter. The structure of fantastic narrative is one founded upon contradictions.

Formalist theories of literary structure, identifying different narrative kinds as corresponding to different linguistic tropes, can be applied to the fantastic. What emerges as the basic trope of fantasy is the *oxymoron*, a figure of speech which holds together contradictions and sustains them in an impossible unity, without progressing towards synthesis. Several literary critics have gestured in more general terms towards this kind of antinomical structure of fantastic texts. 'Fantasy is that kind of extended narrative which establishes and develops an antifact, that is, plays the game of the impossible . . . a fantasy is a story based on and controlled by an overt violation of what is generally accepted as possibility' (Irwin, p.ix).

There is a general agreement that this impossibility is what defines the fantastic as a narrative, though not until Bessière's study was an antinomical structure understood to be a formal determinant. Rabkin claims that 'The truly fantastic occurs when the ground rules of a narrative are forced to make 180 degree reversal, when prevailing perspectives are directly contradicted. . . . The fantastic exists only against a background to which it offers a direct reversal' (pp. 197, 216). The problem with Rabkin's definition is its rigidity: his paradigm is *Alice Through the Looking-Glass*, but more fluid fantasies do not fit his scheme. Other general definitions, such as Caillois's, 'The fantastic is always a break in the acknowledged order, an irruption of the inadmissible within the changeless everyday legality' (*Images, Images*, p.15) do not examine narrative structures. Closest to Bessière's structural definition is Joanna Russ's notion of 'negative subjunctivity':

Fantasy embodies a 'negative subjunctivity' – that is, fantasy is fantasy because it contravenes the real and violates it. The actual world is constantly present in fantasy, by negation . . . fantasy is what *could not have happened*; i.e. what *cannot* happen, what *cannot* exist . . . the negative subjunctivity, the *cannot* or *could not*, constitutes in fact the chief pleasure of fantasy. Fantasy violates the real, contravenes it, denies it, and insists on this denial throughout. (Russ, p.52)

Marcel Brion regards the fantastic as that kind of perception 'qui ouvre sur les plus vastes espaces' (which opens onto the widest spaces) (cit. Hellens, p.67). It is this *opening* activity which is disturbing, by denying the solidity of what had been taken to be real. Bataille has referred to this kind of infraction as 'une déchirure', a tear, or wound, laid open in the side of the real. The same violent 'opening' of syntactic order can be found in Lautréamont, Mallarmé, Rimbaud, Surrealism, Artaud, etc. and from this perspective, fantastic works of the last two centuries are clear antecedents of modernist texts, such as Joyce's *Ulysses* and *Finnegans Wake*, with their commitment to disintegration.

Titles of many fantasies indicate this 'opening' activity, often linking it to notions of (1) invisibility, (2) impossibility, (3) transformation, (4) defiant illusion. For example: (1) Mary Shelley's *The Invisible Girl*, Wells's *The Invisible Man*, Margaret Armstrong's *The Man with no Face*, G.M. Winsor's *Vanishing Men*, E.L. White's *The Man who was not There*, Marcel Aymé's *Le passe-muraille*. (2) Mary Shelley's *The Mortal Immortal*, Arthur Adcock's *The World that Never Was*, John Kendall's *Unborn Tomorrow*, W.O. Stapledon's *Death into Life*, Neal Fyne's *The Land of the Living Dead*, A. Stinger's *The Woman who couldn't die*. (3) Brockden Brown's *Wieland, or The Transformation*, Gautier's *Avatar, or the Double Transformation*, Kafka's *Metamorphosis*, George MacBeth's *The Transformation*. (4) Alfred Noyes's *Walking Shadows*, C.A. Smith's *The Double Shadow*, Abraham Merritt's *Dwellers in the Mirage*, Ursula Le Guin's *The City of Illusions*, William Barrett's *The*

*Shape of Illusion*, *The Shadows of the Images*.

In other works the 'real' world is re-placed, its axis dissolved and distorted so that temporal and spatial structures collapse: F. Anstey's *Vice Versa*, C. Brown's *The Disintegrator*, W. Barrett's *The Edge of Things*, Elizabeth Sewell's *The Dividing of Time*, etc.

Bessière's poetics of fantasy directs attention to the structures behind these themes. The presentation of impossibility is not by itself a radical activity: texts subvert only if the reader is *disturbed* by their dislocated narrative form. The fantastic, as Bessière understands it, cannot be closed off. It lies inside closed systems, infiltrating, opening spaces where unity had been assumed. Its impossibilities propose latent 'other' meanings or realities behind the possible or the known. Breaking single, reductive 'truths', the fantastic traces a space within a society's cognitive frame. It introduces multiple, contradictory 'truths': it becomes polysemic.

> The impossible is a realm of polysemy and of the inscription of another meaning, one which cannot be said. This meaning is produced by a relativizing process which grows out of the play upon ambivalences. Because it is a narrative structured upon contraries, fantasy tells of limits, and it is particularly revealing in pointing to the edges of the 'real'. (Bessière, p.62)

Presenting that which cannot be, but *is*, fantasy exposes a culture's definitions of that which can be: it traces the limits of its epistemological and ontological frame.

Definitions of what can 'be', and images of what cannot be, obviously undergo considerable historical shifts. Non-secularized societies hold different beliefs from secular cultures as to what constitutes 'reality'. Presentations of otherness are imagined and interpreted differently. In what we could call a supernatural economy,[3] otherness is transcendent, marvellously different from the human: the results are religious fantasies of angels, devils, heavens, hells, promised lands, and pagan fantasies of elves, dwarves, fairies, fairyland or 'faery'. In a natural, or secular, economy, otherness is not located elsewhere: it is read as a projection of merely human fears and desires transforming the world through subjective perception. One economy introduces fiction which can be termed 'marvellous', whilst the other produces the 'uncanny' or 'strange'. On the one hand, there are 'marvellous' works which invest otherness with supernatural qualities – magical narratives are of this kind, from *Sir Gawain and the Green Knight* or *The Sleeping Beauty* to *The Lord of the Rings*. On the other hand, there are 'uncanny' stories where strangeness is an effect produced by the distorted and the distorting mind of the protagonist – the evidently hallucinating mind of the narrator of Maupassant's *Horla*, for example:

> I am certain now . . . that an invisible creature exists beside me . . . which can touch things, pick them up and move them about, which is therefore endowed with a material nature, imperceptible though it may be to our senses, and which is living like myself beneath my roof. . . . I would seem to be suffering from hallucinations while remaining perfectly sane.[4]

From Gothic fiction onwards, there is a gradual transition from the marvellous to the uncanny – the history of the survival of Gothic horror is one of progressive internalization and recognition of fears as generated by the self.

It is hardly surprising that the fantastic comes into its own in the nineteenth century, at precisely that juncture when a supernatural 'economy' of ideas was slowly giving way to a natural one, but had not yet been completely displaced by it. Todorov's diagrammatic representation of the changing forms of the fantastic makes this clear: they move from the marvellous (which predominates in a climate of belief in supernaturalism and magic) through the purely fantastic (in which no explanation can be found) to the uncanny (which explains all strangeness as generated by unconscious forces). Thus:

MARVELLOUS ⟶ FANTASY ⟶ UNCANNY

Supernatural        Unnatural        Natural

The fantastic opens on to a region which has no name and no rational explanation for its existence. It suggests events beyond interpretation. As Bessière describes it, amplifying Todorov's scheme: 'Fantastic narrative is presented as a transcription of the imaginary experience of the limits of reason. It links the intellectual falseness of its premises to a hypothesis of the unnatural or supernatural', gradually arriving at a position in which these hypotheses are untenable so that the fantastic introduces 'that which cannot *be*, either in a natural or supernatural economy' (p.62).

During the nineteenth century, then, the fantastic began to hollow out the 'real' world, making it strange, without providing any explanation for the strangeness. Michel Guiomar has termed this effect *l'insolite* – the unusual, the unprecedented – and he has described the negating activity of the fantastic as being one of dissolution, disrepair, disintegration, derangement, dilapidation, sliding away, emptying. The very notion of realism which had emerged as dominant by the mid-nineteenth century is subjected to scrutiny and interrogation.

The fantastic exists as the inside, or underside, of realism, opposing the novel's closed, monological forms with open, dialogical structures, as if the novel had given rise to its own opposite, its unrecognizable reflection. Hence their symbiotic relationship, the axis of one being shaded by the paraxis of the other. The fantastic gives utterance to precisely those elements which are known only through their absence within a dominant 'realistic' order. Fantastic tales proliferate during the nineteenth century as an opposite version of realistic narrative: the literature of the fantastic is 'nothing more than the uneasy conscience of the positivist nineteenth century' (Todorov, p.169). It is all that is not said, all that is unsayable, through realistic forms.

The fantastic is predicated on the category of the 'real', and it introduces areas which can be conceptualized only by negative terms according to the categories of nineteenth century realism: thus, the im-possible, the un-real, the nameless, formless, shapeless, un-known, in-visible. What could be termed a 'bourgeois' category of the real is under attack. It is this *negative relationality* which constitutes the meaning of the modern fantastic.

## The marvellous, mimetic and fantastic

> The distinction between natural and supernatural, in fact, broke down; and when it had done so, one realized how great a comfort it had been – how it had eased the burden of intolerable strangeness which this universe imposes on us.
>
> C.S. Lewis, *Voyage to Venus*

Critics have traditionally defined fantasy in terms of its relation to the 'real', and in literary terms this meant that the fantastic tended to be understood through its relation to realism. Todorov's study was the first to question this classification and to offer a systematic formulation of the poetics of fantasy, which refuses to borrow from extraliterary categories to 'account for' or explain the emergence and existence of the form. Rather than turning too far to philosophical or psychological explanations, Todorov relies upon an analysis of the text in its own terms, so arriving at a theoretical rather than a historical definition of the genre of fantasy. I shall summarize his main ideas before proceeding to suggest a few modifications that might be made.

Given that there seemed to be a common agreement that the fantastic was to do with some kind of existential anxiety and unease, Todorov sought an understanding of *how* literary fantasies produce such an effect. He discovered the kernel of his theories in the writing of a nineteenth-century Russian critic, Vladimir Solovyov, who formulated this definition: 'In the genuine fantastic, there is always the external and formal possibility of a simple explanation of phenomena, but at the same time this explanation is completely stripped of all internal probability.' Interestingly Dostoevsky had arrived at a similar definition himself, when he described Pushkin's tale, *The Queen of Spades* (1834), as 'a masterpiece of fantastic art' in that it was impossible to settle the anxiety aroused by the apparent unreality of events narrated:

> You believe that Herman really had a vision . . . however, at the end of the story, i.e. when you have read it through, *you cannot make up your mind*. Did this vision come out of Herman's nature or was he really one of those who are in contact with another world, one of the evil spirits hostile to mankind? (cit. Linnér, p.179)

True fantasy, according to Dostoevsky, must not break the hesitation experienced by the reader in interpreting events. Tales which are too incredible to be introduced as 'real' break this convention; he dismisses the story of a man with (literally) no heart as mere nonsense, for it breaks the limits of possibility and the agreement between reader and author that the text sets up. 'The fantastic', writes Dostoevsky, 'must be so close to the real that you almost have to believe in it' (p.178).

Todorov saw that Solovyov's definition could be extended into a more rigorous and extensive means of approaching the fantastic. The tale which introduces 'strange' events permits no internal explanation of the strangeness – the protagonist cannot understand what is going on – and this confusion spreads outwards to affect the reader in similar ways. According to Todorov, the purely fantastic text establishes absolute hesitation in protagonist and reader: they can neither come to terms with the unfamiliar events described, nor dismiss them as supernatural phenomena.

Anxiety, then, is not merely a thematic feature, but is incorporated into the *structure* of the work to become its defining element. Todorov insists that it is this systematic writing in, or *inscription*, of hesitation which defines the fantastic.

> The fantastic requires the fulfilment of three conditions. First, the text must oblige the reader to consider the world of the characters as a world of living persons and to hesitate between a natural and supernatural explanation of the events described. Second, this hesitation may also be experienced by a character; thus the reader's role is entrusted to a character . . . the hesitation is represented, it becomes one of the themes of the work. Third, the reader must adopt a certain attitude with regard to the text: he will reject allegorical as well as 'poetic' interpretations. (p.33)

The first and third of these conditions are claimed to constitute the genre, whilst the second is an optional constituent. We can find an example of a tale which incorporates its own scepticism as to the credulity of its contents in Gogol's short story *The Nose* (1836), which influenced Dostoevsky's *The Double*. The narrator deflects the reader's disbelief by confessing to his own and by making explicit the impossibility of understanding the tale in rational terms. The protagonist, Ivan Yakovlevich, discovers 'a very familiar nose' in his morning loaf of bread – a nose which assumes a life of its own. The narrator comments, 'We can see that there is a great deal that is very far-fetched in this story . . . it's *highly* unlikely for a nose to disappear in such a fantastic way and then reappear in various parts of the town dressed as a state councillor.' [5] What is crucial here is that *within the text itself* supernatural and natural explanations of strangeness are made redundant; there is a foregrounding of the impossibility of certainty and of reading in meanings.

Todorov's paradigmatic text is a short story by Cazotte, *Le diable amoreux* (1772), often claimed to be the first purely fantastic tale. Its hero, Alvaro, is in love with a woman called

Biondetta, who turns out to be the devil. Alvaro can never decide who Biondetta is – she is human *and* superhuman, ambiguously both, and drives Alvaro mad with indecision. His inability to define her, to know her, breaks the rational means by which he had ordered the world, and he becomes totally confused as to the nature of the 'real' and his own identity. He is split between a primitive faith in the possibility of supernatural events occurring (Biondetta as the devil) and a deep incredulity that there is anything other than the merely human (Biondetta as a woman). This epistemological uncertainty – often expressed in terms of the madness, hallucination, multiple division of the subject – is a recurrent feature of nineteenth-century fantasy; and as Todorov points out, it is dramatized by the text itself as it produces a similar un-knowingness on the part of the reader. The best example, perhaps, of a fantasy expressing profound uncertainty on the part of the main protagonist (again an uncertainty as to the status of a 'devil' figure) is James Hogg's *Private Memoirs and Confessions of a Justified Sinner*, a work which is literally divided into two sections – one by an editor, one by the confessor – which neatly demonstrate Todorov's theory as to the inscription of double views within the fantastic text.

Hogg's *Confessions* makes it impossible for the reader to arrive at a definitive version of truth. Any accurate account of events, or reliable interpretation, recedes further and further into the distance; or, rather, it is an equivocal truth which is foregrounded as the very subject matter of the tale. Todorov sees this kind of equivocation as one which is produced by a tension between the voice of a 'he' (in Hogg's version, this would be the editor's story) and of an 'I' (this would be the sinner's story). In other words, the hesitation which the story produces is created by a confusion of pronouns and of pronoun functions: the reader is never returned to a position of confidence in relation to the tale such as would be found in a third-person omniscient narrative, where an 'objective', authoritative (authorial) voice, knowing all, tells the meaning of events. Cazotte's story, for example, permits no restoration of certainty for the reader – there is no return to an impersonal voice separate from Alvaro's. The reader is *kept uncertain* as to whether what was given in the name of 'true' experience was true or not. The narrative voice is that of the confused/confusing 'I' at the centre of the tale.

The uncertain vision of the protagonist of the fantastic is spread to the reader through a conflation of narrator and hero. The protagonist's blurred vision and ignorance is the most 'objective' perspective that is possible. And at the same time, it is not possible to distance his experience as being merely the product of his fevered mind, for the narrative voice is frequently a 'he' rather than an 'I', thus ruling out the dismissal of the story as peculiar to that individual mind or subjectivity. The dizzying effect of a tale such as Kafka's *Metamorphosis* derives from this inability to push away the hero's experience as delusory: it is not the dream of an 'I', but the reality of a 'he' in terms of its presentation. Gregor's 'unreal' transformation is 'real': he *is* another being than himself, with his reason intact.

> He would have needed arms and hand to hoist himself up; instead he had only the numerous little legs which never stopped waving in all directions and which he could not control in the least. When he tried to bend one of them it was the first to stretch itself straight . . . he watched his little legs struggling against each other more wildly than ever and saw no way of bringing order into this arbitrary confusion. . . . (pp.12–13)

This confusion between an 'I' and a 'he' through the narrative voice has as its cause and effect an uncertainty of vision, a reluctance or inability to fix things as explicable and known. The fantastic problematizes vision (is it possible to trust the seeing eye?) and language (is it possible to trust the recording, speaking 'I'?). Interestingly, in the translation of a 'fantastic' genre into cinema, these problems are refocused around the vision of the camera 'eye' which can produce similar conflation of 'objective' or documentary recording and an implication of 'subjective' vision through a character in the narrative. Or there can be a presentation of 'unreal' combinations of objects and events as 'real' through the camera eye itself – in this sense, the cinematic process itself could be called 'fantastic'. Mark Nash, writing an analysis of Carl Dreyer's film, *Vampyr*, has drawn attention to the need for a study of the relations and differences between literary and film presentations of the fantastic, and has pointed out that it is the obscuring of a clear vision of a recognizable 'he' or 'I' (with whose eye the reader or spectator can rest secure) that is one of the features common to both.

> The reader's uncertainty as to whether what was given in the name of 'I', of experience, was true or not, suspends his decision as to the register to which he is to assign the pronouns representing the narrating subjectivity. This play with the expectation of coming down one way or the other is far from the open assumption of the separation in the modern text. *It does, however, constitute the play of pronoun functions as a privileged element of the fantastic as a genre.* (Mark Nash, 'Vampyr and the fantastic', p.37)

This problem (and problematization) of the perception/ vision/knowledge of the protagonist and narrator and reader of the fantastic text is not considered by Todorov in any historical perspective, yet it is part of an increasing attention to questions of knowing and seeing which preoccupies much Romantic and post-Romantic thought. Even Todorov's sliding scale of different kinds of fantasy points to its historical contextualization – the purely fantastic, he claims, exists between the purely marvellous (events are supernatural, superhuman, magical) and the purely uncanny (events are understood to be strange because of the deceiving mind of the protagonist). This corresponds to a shift in ideas from supernaturalism towards an increasingly scientific and rationalistic world view. Todorov represents the different kinds of fantasy diagrammatically:

| PURE UNCANNY | FANTASTIC UNCANNY | FANTASTIC MARVELLOUS | PURE MARVELLOUS |
|---|---|---|---|

The area of the pure marvellous indicates narratives such as fairy tales, romance, much science fiction; next to it, the fantastic-marvellous includes works like Théophile Gautier's *La morte amoreuse* and Villiers de l'Isle Adam's *Véra*. These present inexplicable effects which are eventually given supernatural causes. The fantastic-uncanny includes Jan Potocki's *Saragossa Manuscript* (1804), in which strange events are seen as having some subjective origin. Todorov places Poe's tales in the pure uncanny. Closest to his indeterminate, median line of the purely fantastic are Cazotte's *Le Diable Amoreux* and Henry James's *The Turn of the Screw*, where the fantastic occupies a duration of uncertainty, whilst the reader is left in doubt over the origins of 'ghosts' as supernatural or natural presences. The purely fantastic 'may be represented by the median line separating the fantastic-uncanny from the fantastic-marvellous. This line corresponds perfectly to the nature of the fantastic – a frontier between two adjacent realms' (p.44).

This scheme is useful for distinguishing certain kinds of the fantastic, but its polarization of the marvellous and the uncanny leads to some confusion. For to see the fantastic as a literary form, it needs to be made distinct in literary terms, and the uncanny, or *l'étrange*, is not one of these – it is not a literary category, whereas the marvellous is. It is perhaps more helpful to define the fantastic as a literary *mode* rather than a genre, and to place it between the opposite modes of the marvellous and the mimetic. The ways in which it operates can then be understood by its combination of elements of these two different modes.

## The marvellous

The world of fairy story, romance, magic, supernaturalism is one belonging to marvellous narrative. Tales by the Grimm brothers, Hans Andersen, Andrew Lang and Tolkien all belong to this mode. If we take the opening of a story by Grimm, called 'Hans the Hedgehog', we find that the voice is impersonal and that events are distanced well into the past: 'There was once a country man who had money and land in plenty. . . .' [6] Similarly the opening of Charles Kingsley's *Water Babies*: 'Once upon a time there was a little chimney-sweep, and his name was Tom.'[7] These openings are working in similar ways, repeating the formulaic device which opens traditional fairy tales: 'Once upon a time there was. . . .' The narrator is impersonal and has become an authoritative, knowing voice. There is a minimum of emotional involvement in the tale – that voice is positioned with absolute confidence and certainty towards events. It has complete knowledge of *completed* events, its version of history is not questioned and the tale seems to deny the process of its own telling – it is merely reproducing established 'true' versions of what happened. The marvellous is characterized by a minimal functional narrative, whose narrator is omniscient and has absolute authority. It is a form which discourages reader participation, representing events which are in the long distant past, contained and fixed by a long temporal perspective and carrying the implication that their *effects* have long since ceased to disturb. Hence the formulaic ending too, 'and then they lived happily ever after', or a variant upon this. The effect of such narrative is one of a *passive* relation to history. The reader, like the protagonist, is merely a receiver of events which enact a preconceived pattern.

## The mimetic

Narratives which claim to imitate an external reality, which are mimetic (imitating), also distance experience by shaping it into meaningful patterns and sequences. Classic narrative fiction, which is exemplified by so many 'realistic' nineteenth-century novels, represents as 'real' the events it tells, using as mouthpiece a knowing third-person voice. Thus the opening of Thackeray's Victorian novel, *Vanity Fair* (1848): 'On one sunshiny morning in June, there drove up to the great iron gate of Miss Pinkerton's academy for young ladies, on Chiswick Mall, a large family coach....' Or consider Elizabeth Gaskell's 'historical' novel *Mary Barton* (1848): 'There are some fields near Manchester, well known to the inhabitants as "Green Heys Fields", through which runs a public footpath to a little village about two miles distant.' These openings make an implicit claim of equivalence between the represented fictional world and the 'real' world outside the text.

## The fantastic

Fantastic narratives confound elements of both the marvellous and the mimetic. They assert that what they are telling is real – relying upon all the conventions of realistic fiction to do so – and then they proceed to break that assumption of realism by introducing what – within those terms – is manifestly unreal. They pull the reader from the apparent familiarity and security of the known and everyday world into something more strange, into a world whose improbabilities are closer to the realm normally associated with the marvellous. The narrator is no clearer than the protagonist about what is going on, nor about interpretation; the status of what is being seen and recorded as 'real' is constantly in question. This instability of narrative is at the centre of the fantastic as a mode. Thus the circles of equivocation in Poe's stories, such as the opening of 'The black cat':

> For the most wild, yet most homely narrative which I am about to pen, I neither expect nor solicit belief. Mad indeed would I be to expect it, in a case where my very senses

reject their own evidence. Yet, mad am I not – and very surely do I not dream.[8]

Between the marvellous and the mimetic, borrowing the extravagance of one and the ordinariness of the other, the fantastic belongs to neither and is without their assumptions of confidence or presentations of authoritative 'truths'.

It is possible, then, to modify Todorov's scheme slightly and to suggest a definition of the fantastic as a *mode*, which then assumes different generic forms. Fantasy as it emerged in the nineteenth century is one of these forms. It seemed to become a genre in its own right because of its extremely close relation to the form of the novel, a genre which it undermined. As Bakhtin writes, the novel emerged as a form dominated by a secular vision, a narrow monological consciousness, whose view is, 'All that has significance can be collected in a single consciousness and subordinated to a unified accent; everything which is not amenable to such a reduction is accidental and unessential' (p.66). Subverting this unitary vision, the fantastic introduces confusion and alternatives; in the nineteenth century this meant an opposition to bourgeois ideology upheld through the 'realistic' novel.[9]

Lewis Carroll pointed towards this situation of the fantastic as existing between the realistic and the marvellous in his Preface to *Sylvie and Bruno* (1893). Carroll distinguished between three kinds of mental states, which could be seen as related to the three modes (mimetic, fantastic and marvellous) which we have described. The first condition Carroll terms 'ordinary', the second is 'eerie' and the third is 'trance-like'. In an ordinary state of mind, man sees a 'real' world, in an eerie state he sees a 'transitional' world and in a trance-like state he sees an 'imaginary' world. These roughly correspond to mimetic, fantastic and marvellous literary forms. The fantastic exists in the hinterland between 'real' and 'imaginary', shifting the relations between them through its indeterminacy.

A point needs to be made here about the relation between those works which are termed fantastic and those which have been designated surrealistic. Obviously it would be hair-splitting to over-schematize such distinctions, since surrealism has so much in common with fantasy, especially in its use of similar *themes*, such as the disintegration of objects and the fluidity of discrete forms, but there are crucial differences. These are best understood in terms of narrative structure and the relation of the text to the reader. Surrealistic literature is much closer to a marvellous mode in that the narrator himself is rarely in a position of uncertainty. The extraordinary happenings told do not surprise the narrator – indeed he expects them and records them with a bland indifference, a certain neutrality. The opening of a short story by Benjamin Péret, for example, 'A life full of interest', introduces weird events with the same kind of unconcern and authoritative detachment that is to be found in old fairy tales: 'Coming out of her house early in the morning, Mrs Lannor saw that her cherry trees, still covered with fine red fruit the day before, had been replaced during the night by stuffed giraffes.' [10]

The surrealistic then is closer to the marvellous – it is super-real – and its etymology implies that it is presenting a world *above* this one rather than fracturing it from inside or below. Unlike the marvellous or the mimetic, the fantastic is a mode of writing which *enters a dialogue with the 'real' and incorporates that dialogue as part of its essential structure*. To return to Bakhtin's phrase, fantasy is 'dialogical', interrogating single or unitary ways of seeing. The issue of the narrative's internal reality is always relevant to the fantastic, with the result that the 'real' is a notion which is under constant interrogation. The text has not yet become non-referential, as it is in modernist fiction and recent linguistic fantasies (such as some of Borges's stories) which do not question the crucial relation between language and the 'real' world outside the text which the text constructs, so much as move towards another kind of fictional autonomy. The representational means of realism are discovered to be endlessly problematic in many fantasies, from Carroll and Poe to Calvino. They are drawn towards that discourse of the marvellous which Novalis described as 'narrative without coherence but rather with association, like dreams . . . full of words, but without any meaning and coherence . . . like fragments' but they do not escape into it. In their *waking* dreams, it is the strange relation between the 'real' and its representation which is their concern.

## Non-signification

The literature of the fantastic leaves us with two notions – reality and literature – each one as unsatisfactory as the other.

Todorov, *The Fantastic*

A reluctance, or an inability, to present definitive versions of 'truth' or 'reality' makes of the modern fantastic a literature which draws attention to its own practice as a linguistic system. Structured upon contradiction and ambivalence, the fantastic traces in that which cannot be said, that which evades articulation or that which is represented as 'untrue' and 'unreal'. By offering a problematic re-presentation of an empirically 'real' world, the fantastic raises questions of the nature of the real and unreal, foregrounding the relation between them as its central concern. It is in this sense that Todorov refers to fantasy as the most 'literary' of all literary forms, as 'the quintessence of literature', for it makes explicit the problems of establishing 'reality' and 'meaning' through a literary text. As Bessière writes, 'Fantastic narrative is perhaps the most artificial and deliberate mode of literary narrative . . . it is constructed on the affirmation of emptiness . . . uncertainty arises from this mixture of too much and of nothing' (p.34).

The impossibility of verification of events, found in Hoffmann's tales and in Hogg's *Confessions*, becomes central to post-Romantic fantasies. Perception becomes increasingly confused, signs are vulnerable to multiple and contradictory interpretation, so that 'meanings' recede indefinitely, with 'truth' as a mere vanishing point of the text. Bellemin-Noël's critique of Todorov argues that it is this lack of meaningful signification which is the major defining feature of the fantastic, being of equal importance to structural equivocation and suggesting the same trouble in representing or reaching a 'real', absolute signified. Bellemin-Noël claims that:

> one could talk of a rhetoric of the *unsayable* . . . the fantastic activity often returns to a creation of 'pure signifiers' . . . All these lexical units, marked by a sort of 'insignification' on the communicative level of language, do have some kind of signified, but it is an approximate one: one could say that they signify by connoting without denoting; or that, failing to be circumscribed by a definition, they install a (short)-signifying-circuit because they are connected up with a network of limitless images. (my translation, pp. 112–13)

That gap between sign and meaning which has become a dominant concern of modernism is anticipated by many post-Romantic works in a fantasy mode. Samuel Beckett's *Molloy* (1959), registering a final disjunction between word and object – 'There could be no things but nameless things, no names but thingless names' – is an expression of a severance of connecting lines of meaning, a severance given graphic form in many fantasies. A gap between signifier and signified works both ways in the modern fantastic. On the one side, there is a presentation of 'nameless things'. In nineteenth century tales of fantasy and horror, from MacDonald's *Lilith* and *Phantastes*, Bulwer Lytton's *Zanoni* and *Strange Story*, Maupassant's *Horla* and *He*, to Poe's stories and the beginning of Stoker's *Dracula*, there is an apprehension of something unnameable: the 'It', the 'He', the 'thing', the 'something', which can have no adequate articulation except through suggestion and implication. H.P. Love-craft's horror fantasies are particularly self-conscious in their stress on the impossibility of naming this unnameable pre-sence, the 'thing' which can be registered in the text only as absence and shadow. (In film, the 'unseen' has a similar function.) Lovecraft's *The Mountains of Madness* (1939), for example, circles around this dark area in an attempt to get beyond language to something other, yet the endeavour to visualize and verbalize the unseen and unsayable is one which inevitably falls short, except by drawing attention to exactly this difficulty of utterance:

> The words reaching the reader can never suggest the awfulness of the sight itself. It crippled our consciousness completely . . . What we did see . . . was the utter objective embodiment of the fantastic novelist's 'thing that should not be' . . . a terrible, indescribable thing. (pp. 106–7)[11]

Lovecraft's fragmented story *The Transition of Juan Romero* works similarly, leading to a climax which declares itself as impossibility:

> In that moment it seemed as if all the hidden terrors and monstrosities of earth had become articulate in an effort to overwhelm the human race . . . I had arrived at the abyss . . . I peered over the edge of that chasm which no light could fathom . . . At first I beheld nothing but a seething blur of luminosity; but then shapes, all infinitely distant, began to detach themselves from the confusion, and I saw . . . but God! I dare not tell you what I saw! . . . Some power from heaven, coming to my aid, obliterated both sights and sounds in such a crash as may be heard when two universes collide in space.[12]

Lovecraft's ghost and horror fiction makes explicit the prob-lem of naming all that is 'other', all that is designated 'unreal' by what he derides as 'prosaic materialism,' and 'the common veil of obvious empiricism'. 'I am not even certain how I am communicating this message. While I know I am speaking, I have a vague impression that some strange and perhaps terrible mediation will be needed to bear what I say to the points where I wish to be heard.' [13]

On the other side of Beckett's formulation lie 'thingless names', also recurring in the fantastic as words which are apprehended as empty signs, without meaning. Lewis Carroll's *Alice* books and his *Hunting of the Snark* and *Sylvie and Bruno* reveal his reliance upon portmanteau words and nonsense utterances as a shift towards language as signifying nothing, and the fantastic itself as such a language. His snark, boojum, jabberwocky, uggug, like Poe's Tekeli-li, Dostoevsky's 'bobok', or Lovecraft's Cthulhu, Azathoth, Nyarlathotep, are all mere signifiers without an object. They are inverted and invented 'nonsense' (non-sense) words, indicating nothing but their proper density and excess. The signifier is not secured by the weight of the signified: it begins to float free. Whereas the gap between signifier and signified is closed in 'realistic' narrative (as it is in classic narrative cinema), in fantastic literature (and in the cine-fantastic) it is left open. The relation of sign to meaning is hollowed out, anticipating that kind of semiotic excess which is found in modernist texts. From Carroll, through Kafka, to modern writers such as J.L. Borges in *Labyrinths* there is a progressive dissolution of any predictable or reliable relation between signifier and signified. Fantasy becomes a literature of separation, of discourse without an object, foreshadowing that explicit focus upon problems of literature's signifying activity found in modern anti-realist texts.

Sartre's essay on Maurice Blanchot's early Kafka-esque fantasy, *Aminadab* (referred to previously) defines the modern fantastic as a *language* of peculiarly empty utterances, of non-signifying signs. These signs, claims Sartre, no longer lead anywhere. They represent nothing, compelling recognition only through their own density. They are means without ends, signs, tokens, signifiers, which are superficially full, but which lead to a terrible emptiness. The 'object' world of the fantastic, found, for example, in Kafka's fiction, is one of semiotic excess and of semantic vacuity. Thus Sartre writes of this world as being one which is pregnant with emptiness:

> The law of the fantastic condemns it to encounter instruments only. These instruments are not . . . meant to serve men, but rather to manifest unremittingly an evasive, preposterous finality. This accounts for the labyrinth of corridors, doors and staircases that lead to nothing, the signposts that lead to nothing, the innumerable signs that line the road and that mean nothing. In the 'topsy-turvy' world, the means is isolated and is posed for its own sake. (p.62)

The fantastic, then, pushes towards an area of non-signification. It does this either by attempting to articulate 'the unnameable', the 'nameless things' of horror fiction, attempting to visualize the unseen, or by establishing a disjunction of word and meaning through a play upon 'thing-less names'. In both cases, the gap between signifier and signified dramatizes the impossibility of arriving at definitive meaning, or absolute 'reality'. As Todorov points out, the fantastic cannot be placed alongside allegory nor poetry, for it resists both the conceptualizations of the first and the metaphorical structures of the second. It tends towards the non-conceptual, or pre-conceptual. (As Blanchot puts it, 'the quest of literature is the quest for the moment which precedes it'.) When it is 'naturalized' as allegory or symbolism, fantasy loses its proper non-signifying nature. Part of its subversive power lies in this resistance to allegory and metaphor. For it takes metaphorical constructions literally. Donne's famous metaphor 'I am every dead thing', for example, is literally realized in Mary Shelley's *Frankenstein*, and in Romero's film *Night of the Living Dead*. It could be suggested that the movement of fantastic narrative is one of *metonymical* rather than of *metaphorical* process: one object does not *stand for* another, but literally becomes that other, slides into it, metamorphosing from one shape to another in a permanent flux and instability. As Lacan has pointed out, 'What do we have in metonymy other than the power to bypass the obstacles of social censure? This form . . . lends itself to the truth under oppression.'[14] The fact that most fantasies recuperate or naturalize this process by pulling their narratives into conceptual, often quasi-allegorical or romance structures (as in *Dracula*, or *Jekyll and Hyde*, or Peake's *Gormenghast* trilogy) indicates the disturbing thrust of the fantastic in its resistance to the endings and meanings of closed, 'signifying' narratives.

## Topography, themes, myths

> Hell is the place of those who have denied;
> They find there what they planted and what dug,
> A Lake of Spaces, and a Wood of Nothing,
> And wander there and drift, and never cease
> Wailing for substance.
>
> W.B. Yeats, *The Hour-Glass*

The topography, themes and myths of the fantastic all work together to suggest this movement towards a realm of non-signification, towards a zero point of non-meaning. The represented world of the fantastic is of a different kind from the imagined universe of the marvellous and it opposes the latter's rich, colourful fullness with relatively bleak, empty, indeterminate landscapes, which are less definable as places than as spaces, as white, grey, or shady blanknesses. Movement into a *marvellous* realm transports the reader or viewer into an absolutely different, alternative world, a 'secondary' universe, as Auden and Tolkien term it.[15] This secondary, duplicated cosmos, is relatively autonomous, relating to the 'real' only through metaphorical reflection and never, or rarely, intruding into or interrogating it. This is the place of William Morris's *The Wood Beyond the World*, Frank Baum's

*Wonderful Land of Oz*, C.S. Lewis's *Narnia*, Fritz Leiber's *Nehwon*, Tolkien's Middlearth in *The Lord of the Rings*, Frank Herbert's *Dune*, the realms of fairy story and of much science fiction.

Such marvellous narratives have a tangential relation to the 'real', interrogating its values only retrospectively or allegorically. Ursula Le Guin's science fiction fantasies, for example, construct a whole galactic civilization through a number of planets incorporating different aspects of human culture, magnifying certain features and diminishing others. They build up *another* universe out of elements of this one, according to dystopian fears and utopian desires, rather like Swift's satirical methods in *Gulliver's Travels*. Their other world, however new or strange, is linked to the real through an allegorical association, as an exemplification of a possibility to be avoided or embraced. The basic relation is a conceptual one, a linking through ideas and ideals. The fantastic, by contrast, is moving towards the non-conceptual. Unlike faery, it has little faith in ideals, and unlike science fiction, it has little interest in ideas. Instead, it moves into, or opens up, a space without /outside cultural order.

The notion of 'paraxis' introduced optic imagery in relation to the fantastic and it is useful to return to it in considering topography, for many of the strange worlds of modern fantasy are located in, or through, or beyond, the mirror. They are spaces behind the visible, behind the image, introducing dark areas from which anything can emerge.

The topography of the modern fantastic suggests a preoccupation with problems of vision and visibility, for it is structured around spectral imagery: it is remarkable how many fantasies introduce mirrors, glasses, reflections, portraits, eyes – which see things myopically, or distortedly, or out of focus – to effect a transformation of the familiar into the unfamiliar. E.T.A. Hoffmann's *The Sandman* derives its dislocated sense of the 'real' from the confused vision of its protagonist Nathaniel, whose apprehensions, terrors and phobias are all related to his *eyes*: the fear of loss of sight, of no longer being able to see (and so control) things clearly is at the centre of the tale. Many Victorian fantasies employ the device of a lens or mirror to introduce an indeterminate area where distortions and deformations of 'normal' perception become the norm. Lewis Carroll's Alice moves *through* the looking-glass into a paraxial realm, where anything can happen. 'Let's pretend the glass has got all soft like gauze, so that we can get through. Why, it's turning into a sort of mist now . . . It'll be easy enough to get through.' [16]

Similarly, George MacDonald's fantasies rely heavily upon mirrors, portraits, doors, apertures which open into another region found in the spaces of the familiar and the known. Vane, the narcissistic hero of *Lilith*, has access to his imaginary realm through the mirror in his bedroom, 'I touched the glass; it was impermeable . . . I shifted and shifted the mirrors . . . until at last . . . things came right between them . . . I stepped forward, and my feet were among the heather'.[17] Not only mirrors, but all apertures lead Vane elsewhere. 'How could I any longer call that house *home*', he asks, 'where every door, every window opened into − Out'.[18] All openings transport him into 'a world very much another than this'. H.G. Wells's short story *The Door in the Wall* (1906) contains a 'real' door leading a man to 'immortal realities', hidden 'in the margin of his field of vision'. It promises him an unknown life, as he grows older '*coveting*, passionately desiring, the green door'.[19] Another example of this entrance into a fantastic landscape via an aperture or reflection is Valery Brussof's strange tale *The Mirror* (1918). Here, a woman loses her identity when she is literally replaced by her mirror image and she herself steps through into the area behind the mirror, an area she describes as 'this protracted actuality, separated from us by the smooth surface of glass, [which] drew me towards itself by a kind of intangible touch, dragged me forward, as to an abyss, a mystery'.[20]

Frequently, the mirror is employed as a motif or device to introduce a double, or *Döppelganger* effect: the reflection in the glass is the subject's other, as in R.L. Stevenson's *Dr Jekyll and Mr Hyde*: 'when I looked upon that ugly idol in the glass, I was conscious of no repugnance, rather of a leap of welcome. This, too, was myself. It seemed natural and human.'[21] The painted portrait in Wilde's *Picture of Dorian Gray* functions similarly, as an iconographical establishment of difference, illustrating self as other, and suggesting the inseparability of these devices and mirror images from fantastic themes of duplicity and multiplicity of selves.

Unlike marvellous secondary worlds, which construct alternative realities, the shady worlds of the fantastic construct nothing. They are empty, emptying, dissolving. Their emptiness vitiates a full, rounded, three-dimensional visible world, by tracing in absences, shadows without objects. Far from fulfilling desire, these spaces perpetuate desire by insisting upon *absence*, lack, the non-seen, the unseeable. The seeker of Italo Calvino's abstract fantasy *Invisible Cities* (1972), for example, declares the impossibility of fulfilment: invisibility, or threatened invisibility, removes certainty and disturbs the premises and the promises of the 'real': 'Elsewhere', he writes, 'is a negative mirror. The traveller recognizes the little that is his, discovering the much he has not had and never will have.'[22]

An emphasis upon invisibility points to one of the central thematic concerns of the fantastic: problems of vision. In a culture which equates the 'real' with the 'visible' and gives the eye dominance over other sense organs, the un-real is that which is in-visible. That which is not seen, or which threatens to be un-seeable, can only have a subversive function in relation to an epistemological and metaphysical system which makes 'I see' synonymous with 'I understand'. Knowledge, comprehension, reason, are established through the power of the *look*, through the *'eye'* and the *'I'* of the human subject whose relation to objects is structured through his field of vision. In fantastic art, objects are not readily appropriated through the look: things slide away from the powerful eye/I which seeks to possess them, thus becoming distorted, disintegrated, partial and lapsing into invisibility.

From about 1800 onwards, one of the most frequent landscapes of fantasy has been the hollow world, one which is surrounded by the real and the tangible, but which is itself empty, mere absence. William Morris's *The Hollow Land* (1856), for example, narrates a quest for an area known only by its insubstantiality and difference, somewhere approached through the interstices of solid things, 'between the rift of rocks'. Morris's protagonist seeks this hollow region as being a realm before time, before separation into self and other, before the establishment of distinct identities or genders, before the 'fall' into difference and a consciousness of ego, of the 'I': 'Yet beyond, oh such a land! . . . a great hollow land . . . reaches and reaches of loveliest country . . . I know, that *we* abode continually in the Hollow Land until *I* lost it! [23] (The shifting pronouns here, making the loss equivalent with a progression from *we* to *I*, indicate that the ideal, imaginary, hollow land is a realm of integration, preceding separateness and division of self from other.)

Classical unities of space, time and character are threatened with dissolution in fantastic texts. Perspective art and three-dimensionality no longer hold as ground rules: parameters of the field of vision tend towards indeterminacy, like the shifting edges of Kafka's *The Burrow*, or the infinitely receding passages and labyrinthine extensions of Mervyn Peake's *Gormenghast* and Borges's *Labyrinths*, or the soluble walls of Ursula Le Guin's *City of Illusions*. It is as though 'the limited nature of space', to which Kant referred in his *Distinctions of Regions in Space* (1768), had inserted into it an additional dimension, where 'incongruent counterparts' can co-exist and where that transformation which Kant called 'a turning over of a left hand into a right hand' can be effected. This additional space is frequently narrowed down into a place, or *enclosure*, where the fantastic has become the norm. Enclosures are central to modern fantasy, from the dark, threatening edifices and castles of Gothic fiction and Sade's *120 Days of Sodom*, through the threatening architecture of nineteenth-century tales of terror, to new enclosures of metropolitan nightmare in Dickens, Kafka and Pynchon. Poe's *House of Usher*, Stoker's *Dracula,* Faulkner's *Sanctuary,* Hitchcock's *Psycho*, etc., all rely upon the Gothic enclosure as a space of maximum transformation and terror.

Chronological time is similarly exploded, with time past, present and future losing their historical sequence and tending towards a suspension, an eternal present. 'My memories are very confused. There is even much doubt as to where they begin; for at times I feel appalling vistas of years stretching behind me, while at other times it seems as if the present moment were an isolated point in a grey, formless infinity . . . just what the year was, I cannot say; for since then I have known many ages and dimensions, and have had all my notions of time dissolved and refashioned.'[24] Fantasies of immortality, increasingly popular in post-Romantic fiction, conflate different temporal scales so that centuries, years, months, days, hours and minutes appear as arbitrary and insubstantial units which, like Salvador Dali's dissolving watches, are made flexible and fluid. C.R. Maturin's *Melmoth the Wanderer* moves through time, his days a society's decades; Mary Shelley's Wandering Jew of *The Mortal Immortal* is outside time, unable to be located within a familiar temporal structure.[25] Time is indefinitely suspended in Nerval's *Aurélia* in a chapter urging 'Do not believe chronometers: time is dead; henceforth there will be no more years, nor months, nor hours; Time is dead and we are walking in its funeral procession.'[26] A gradual seduction into a fantastic landscape is made equivalent with a loss of chronological sequence in many texts: Bram Stoker's *Dracula* witnesses Jonathan Harker's meticulous time-keeping ('3 May. Bistritz – left Munich at 8.35 p.m., on 1st May, arriving at Vienna early next morning; should have arrived at 6.46, but train was an hour late . . . I feared to go very far from the station, as we had arrived late and would start as near the correct time as possible') gradually made ineffective in measuring or charting events ('It seems to me that the further east you go the more unpunctual are the trains.') [27]

Kafka's *Metamorphosis* slowly erases clock time as the intervals between episodes (marked by hours and minutes) expand and become central. With time, as with space, it is the intervals between things which come to take precedence in the fantastic: part of its transformative power lies in this radical shift of vision from units, objects, and fixities, to the intervals between them, attempting to see as things the spaces between things.

Themes of the fantastic in literature revolve around this problem of making visible the un-seen, of articulating the un-said. Fantasy establishes, or dis-covers, an absence of separating distinctions, violating a 'normal', or common-sense perspective which represents reality as constituted by discrete but connected units. Fantasy is preoccupied with limits, with limiting categories, and with their projected dissolution. It subverts dominant philosophical assumptions which uphold as 'reality' a coherent, single-viewed entity, that narrow vision which Bakhtin termed 'monological'. It would be impossible to arrive at a comprehensive list of all the various semantic features of the fantastic, but it is possible to see its thematic elements as deriving from the same source: a dissolution of separating categories, a fore-grounding of those spaces which are hidden and cast into/as darkness, by the placing and naming of the 'real' through chronological temporal structures and three-dimensional spatial organization.

That inscription of hesitation on the level of narrative *structure*, which Todorov identified as fantasy's defining feature, can be read as a displacement of fantasy's central *thematic* issue: an uncertainty as to the nature of the 'real', a problematization of categories of 'realism' and 'truth', of the 'seen' and 'known' (in a culture which declares 'seeing is believing'). Fantasy's ambiguous literary effects, on the level of form, enact its thematic uncertainties and hesitations, through a sliding of thematic into structural equivocation.

Themes can be clustered into several related areas: (1) invisibility, (2) transformation, (3) dualism, (4) good versus evil. These generate a number of recurrent motifs: ghosts, shadows, vampires, werewolves, doubles, partial selves, reflections (mirrors), enclosures, monsters, beasts, cannibals. Transgressive impulses towards incest, necrophilia, androgyny, cannibalism, recidivism, narcissism and 'abnormal' psychological states conventionally categorized as hallucination, dream, insanity, paranoia, derive from these thematic concerns, all of them concerned with erasing rigid demarcations of gender and of genre. Gender differences of male and of female are subverted and generic distinctions between animal, vegetable and mineral are blurred in fantasy's attempt to 'turn over' 'normal' perceptions and undermine 'realistic' ways of seeing.

Uncertainty and impossibility are inscribed on a structural level through hesitation and equivocation, and on a thematic level through images of formlessness, emptiness and invisibility. That which is not seen, that which is not said, is not 'known' and it remains as a threat, as a dark area from which any object or figure can enter at any time. The relation of the individual subject to the world, to others, to objects, ceases to be known or safe, and problems of apprehension (in the double sense of perceiving and of fearing) become central to the modern fantastic. A text such as James Hogg's *Private Memoirs and Confessions of a Justified Sinner* graphically depicts the emergence of this difficult relation of self to world in fantasies of the late Romantic period. The subject's relation to the phenomenal world is made problematical and the text foregounds the impossibility of definitive interpretation or vision: everything becomes equivocal, blurred, 'double', out of focus.

At the heart of this confusion is the problematic relation

of self to other, the 'I' and the 'not-I', the 'I' and the 'you'. Todorov divides the contents of fantastic literature into two groups: the first dealing with themes of the 'I', and the second dealing with themes of the 'not-I'. Fantasies in the first group are constructed around the relationship of the individual to the world, with the structuring of that world through the I, the consciousness which sees (through the eye), perceives, interprets, and places self in relation to a world of objects. This relation is a difficult one in the fantastic: vision can never be trusted, senses prove to be deceptive, and the equation of 'I' with the seeing 'eye' proves to be an untrustworthy, indeed frequently a fatal affair.

Fantasies of subjective dislocation exemplify this problematic relationship of self to world (Hogg's *Confessions*, Hoffmann's *The Sandman*, Nerval's *Aurélia*, Maupassant's *Horla*). Their subjects are unable to separate ideas from perceptions, or to distinguish differences between self and world. Ideas become visible, palpable, so that mind and body, mind and matter merge together. As Todorov notes, 'a generating principle of all the themes collected in this first system [is that]: the transition from mind to matter has become possible'. Behind metamorphosis (self becoming another, whether animal or vegetable) and pan-determinism (everything has its cause and fits into a cosmic scheme, a series in which nothing is by chance, everything corresponds to the subject), the same principle operates, in a sense of correspondence, of sameness, of a collapse of differences. Doubles, or multiple selves, are manifestations of this principle: the *idea* of multiplicity is no longer a metaphor, but is literally realized, self transforms into selves. 'The multiplication of personality, taken literally, is an immediate consequence of the possible transition between matter and mind: we are several persons mentally, we become so physically' (Todorov, p.116). Other persons and objects are no longer distinctly other: the limit between subject and object is effaced, things slide into one another, in a metonymical action of replacement. Todorov cites

Gautier: 'By a strange miracle, after a few moments' contemplation, I dissolved into the object I gazed at, and I myself became that object.'

All these thematic clusters revolve around difficulties of perception and knowledge: the question of vision and the control of the 'eye'/'I' of the subject. From ambiguities of vision derive all those thematic elements associated with fantastic narratives focussed upon the self, the 'I', and his/her problematic differentiation from the 'not-I'. To quote Todorov:

> the principle we have discovered may be designated as the fragility of the limit between matter and mind. This principle engenders several fundamental themes: a special causality, pan-determinism; multiplication of the personality; collapse of the limit between subject and object; and lastly, the transformation of time and space . . . this list collects the essential elements of the basic network of fantastic themes . . . 'of the self'. (p.120)

Fantasies in the second group are structured around the 'not-I'. In Mark Nash's words, this second class concerns

> the dynamic relations of human action in the world through the mediation of others, and are characterized in the fantastic through themes of discourse and desire, the latter in excessive forms as well as in its various transformations (perversions) in themes of cruelty, violence, death, life after death, corpses, and vampires. (Nash, '*Vampyr* and the fantastic', p.65)

Whereas themes of the self, the 'I', deal with problems of *consciousness*, of vision and perception, themes of the other, the 'not-I', deal with problems generated by desire, by the *unconscious*. The relation of self to other is mediated through desire, and fantastic narratives in this category tell of various versions of that desire, usually in transgressive forms. Sadism, incest, necrophilia, murder, eroticism, make explicit the unconscious desires structuring interrelationship, the interactions of 'I' and 'not-I' on a human level. Todorov insists upon the centrality of language in this cluster of fantastic themes, for it is language which structures relationship: 'themes of discourse' are inextricably bound up with these 'themes of the other', just as 'themes of vision' are bound up with 'themes of the self'.

Various motifs, then, are variations upon these basic semantic elements of the 'I' and the 'not-I', and of their interrelations. One of the central thrusts of the fantastic is an attempt to erase this distinction itself, to resist separation and difference, to re-discover a unity of self and other. Its attempts to establish a state of undifferentiation, of unity of self and not-self, reveals itself differently in different periods. In order to contextualize the modern fantastic, it is worth considering a few determining factors and pointing out some contrasts with older forms of fantasy.

Fantasy has always provided a clue to the limits of a culture, by foregrounding problems of categorizing the 'real' and of the situation of the self in relation to that dominant notion of 'reality'. As Fredric Jameson argues in his article, 'Magical narratives: romance as genre', it is the identification, the naming of otherness, which is a telling index of a society's religious and political beliefs.

The concept of evil, which is usually attached to the other, is relative, transforming with shifts in cultural fears and values. Any social structure tends to exclude as 'evil' anything radically different from itself or which threatens it with destruction, and this conceptualization, this naming of difference as evil, is a significant ideological gesture. It is a concept 'at one with the category of otherness itself: evil characterizes whatever is radically different from me, whatever by virtue of precisely that difference seems to constitute a very real and urgent threat to my existence' (Jameson, p.140). A stranger, a foreigner, an outsider, a social deviant, anyone speaking in an unfamiliar language or acting in unfamiliar ways, anyone whose origins are unknown or who has extraordinary powers, tends to be set apart as other, as evil. Strangeness precedes the naming of it as evil: the other is defined as evil precisely because of his/her difference and a possible power to disturb the familiar and the known.

Namings of otherness in fantasies betray the ideological assumptions of the author and of the culture in which they originate, and Jameson emphasizes the need for understanding these identifications, since they *inscribe* social values within the text, often in hidden or obscure ways, for the link between the individual work and its context is a deep, unspoken one.

> Any analysis of romance as a mode will then want to come to terms with the intimate and constitutive relationship between the form itself, as a genre and a literary institution, and this deep-rooted ideology which has only too clearly the function of drawing the boundaries of a given social order and providing a powerful internal deterrent against deviancy or subversion. (Jameson, p.140)

In its broadest sense, fantastic literature has always been concerned with revealing and exploring the interrelations of the 'I' and the 'not-I', of self and other. Within a supernatural economy, or a magical thought mode, otherness is designated as otherworldly, supernatural, as being above, or outside, the human. The other tends to be identified as an otherworldly, evil force: Satan, the devil, the demon (just as good is identified through figures of angels, benevolent fairies, wise men). In religious fantasies and in pagan ones, this context of supernaturalism/magic locates good and evil *outside* the merely human, in a different dimension. It is a displacement of human responsibility on to the level of destiny: human action is seen as operating under the controlling influence of Providence, whether for good or for evil.

Early romance fantasies define and confine otherness as evil and diabolic: difference is located 'out there', in a

supernatural creature. Histories of a devil figure in literature point to its supernatural categorization in religious
myth, medieval romances, fairy tale: disembodied evil came
to be incarnated in a traditional black devil. Blackness, night,
darkness always surrounded this 'other', this unseen presence, outside the forms and visible confines of the 'ordinary' and 'common'. Narratives of diabolism, as Bessière
argues, are still crucial indices of cultural limits: they might
seem empty discourses now, but they are still pertinent, for
they return us to an encounter with that area which has been
'silenced by culture'.

One of the namings of otherness has been as 'demonic'
and it is important to recognize the semantic shifts of this
term, since they indicate the progressive internalization
of fantastic narrative in the post-Romantic period. J.A.
Symonds saw all fantastic art as characterized by an obsession
with the demonic. He referred to Shakespeare's Caliban,
Milton's Death, and Goethe's Mephistopheles as 'products
of fantastic art', and in earlier fantasies it is easy to see that
the demonic and the diabolic were more or less synonymous. The term *demonic* originally denoted a supernatural
being, a ghost, or spirit, or genius, or devil and it usually
connoted a malignant, destructive force at work.

The modern fantastic is characterized by a radical shift in
the naming, or interpretation, of the demonic. One of the
signs of this shift is a transformation in the use of the
demonic in the Faust myth, one of the most widely disseminated fictions exemplifying the relation between man and
'devil'. Whereas Marlowe's *Doctor Faustus* (1596–1604) had
introduced demons who appeared on stage to drag Faustus
to hell – the reward for having sold his soul for impossible
knowledge – versions of Faust from the late eighteenth
century onwards are much more equivocal, much less able
to locate the devil 'out there', apart from the subject. Many
Romantic texts are structured around Faustian themes and
figures, but they increasingly hesitate between supernatural
and natural explanations of the devil's genesis, often inscrib-

ing this split between transcendentalist and humanistic reasoning into the text itself. Charles Brockden Brown's *Wieland, or the Transformation* (1798), Chamisso's *Peter Schlemihl* (1813), C.R. Maturin's *Melmoth the Wanderer* (1820), James Hogg's *Private Memoirs and Confessions of a Justified Sinner* (1824), E.T.A. Hoffmann's *Elixirs of the Devil* (1813–16), Cazotte's *Le Diable Amoreux* (1772), all revolve around demonic pacts, yet equivocate as to the nature of the demonic. They give an impression of uncertainty as to the genesis of the dark 'other', introducing doubt as to whether it is self-generated, or undoubtedly external to the subject.

Over the course of the nineteenth century, fantasies structured around dualism – often variations of the Faust myth – reveal the *internal* origin of the other. The demonic is not supernatural, but is an aspect of personal and interpersonal life, a manifestation of unconscious desire. Around such narratives, themes of the 'I' and the 'not-I' interact strangely, expressing difficulties of knowledge (of the 'I') (introducing problems of *vision*) and of guilt, over desire, (relation to the 'not-I') articulated in the narrative (introducing problems of *discourse*), the two intertwining with each other, as in *Frankenstein*. Mary Shelley's *Frankenstein* is the first of many fantasies re-deploying a Faustian tale on a fully *human* level. From then onwards, fantastic narratives are clearly secularized: the 'other' is no longer designated as supernatural, but is an externalization of part of the self. The text is structured around a dialogue between self and self *as* other, articulating the subject's relation to cultural law and to established 'truths', the truths of the establishment. By the time of Heine's version of Faust, the supernatural reading of the demonic is made uneasy: Faust is mocked by demons whispering, 'we always appear in the shape of your most secret thoughts', and by the time of Dostoevsky, the function of the demonic as a projection of an unconscious part of the self is confirmed. Dostoevsky's *The Possessed* and *Brothers Karamazov* represent the 'devil' as self assuming the voice of another, thus Ivan Karamazov rebuking his demon:

It's I, *I myself, speaking, not you* . . . Never for one minute
have I taken you for reality . . . You are a lie, you are my
illness, you are a phantom . . . You are my hallucination.
You are the incarnation of myself . . . it is really I myself
who appear in different forms.[28]

Because of this progressive internalization of the
demonic, the easy polarization of good and evil which had
operated in tales of supernaturalism and magic ceased to be
effective. Romance narratives, especially classic fairy tales,
represented all action unfolding under the influence of
good or evil powers, with persons in the drama functioning
as mere agents of this metaphysical battle. A loss of faith in
supernaturalism, a gradual scepticism and problematization of the relation of self to world, introduced a much
closer 'otherness', something intimately related to the self.
During the Romantic period, the sense of the 'demonic' was
slowly modified from a supernatural meaning into something more disturbing, something less definable. Goethe's
articulation of this demonism is apposite to an understanding of the modern fantastic, in its apprehension of otherness
as a force which is neither good, nor evil. In his autobiogra-
phy, Goethe writes:

He thought he could detect in nature – both animate and
inanimate, with soul or without soul – something which
manifests itself only in contradictions, and which, therefore, could not be comprehended under any idea, still
less under one word. It was not godlike, for it seemed
unreasonable; not human, for it had no understanding;
nor devilish, for it was beneficent; nor angelic, for it often
betrayed a malicious pleasure. It resembled chance, for it
evolved no consequences; it was like Providence, for it
hinted at connection. All that limits us it seemed to penetrate; it seemed to sport at will with the necessary elements of our existence; it contracted time and expanded
space. To this principle . . . I gave the name of *Demonic*
. . . (Goethe, p.321)

Goethe's *Faust* (1808) moves towards this apprehension of the demonic as a realm of non-signification. His Mephistopheles is much more complex than a stock representation of evil: 'he' introduces a negation of cultural order, insisting that there is no absolute meaning in the world, no value, and that beneath natural phenomena, all that can be dis-covered is a sinister *absence of meaning*. 'His' 'demonic' enterprise consists in revealing this absence, exposing the world's concealed vacuity, emptiness, and its latent pull towards disorder and undifferentiation. Thomas Mann's *Doctor Faustus* (1947) employs the Faust myth in a similar way: the 'demonic' spirit is one which reveals everything as 'its own parody', and which sees through forms to the formlessness they conceal. Through Leverkühn, the artist, a demonic voice calls nature 'illiterate', mere vacancy, and the universe a space filled with signs deprived of meanings. Transformations of the Faust myth epitomize the semantic changes undergone by fantasy in literature within a progressively secularized culture. The demonic pact which Faust makes signifies a desire for absolute knowledge, for a realization of impossibility, transgressing temporal, spatial and personal limitations, becoming as God. But this desire is represented as increasingly tragic, futile and parodic. In a general shift from a supernatural to a natural economy of images, the demonic pact comes to be synonymous with an impossible desire to break human limits, it becomes a *negative version* of desire for the infinite. In the modern fantastic, this desire expresses itself as a violent transgression of all human limitations and social taboos prohibiting the realization of desire. In these versions of Faust, the naming of the demonic reveals a progressive pull towards a recognition of otherness as neither supernatural nor evil but as that which is *behind*, or *between*, separating forms and frames. 'Otherness' is all that threatens 'this' world, this 'real' world, with dissolution: and it is this opposition which lies behind the several myths which have developed in the modern fantastic.

Starting from Todorov's identification of two groups of fantastic themes, those dealing with the 'I' and those dealing with the 'not-I', or the 'other', it is possible to see two kinds of myths in the modern fantastic. In the first, the source of otherness, of threat, is in the *self*. Danger is seen to originate from the subject, through excessive knowledge, or rationality, or the mis-application of the human will. This pattern would be exemplified by *Frankenstein*, and is repeated in H.G. Wells's *The Island of Dr Moreau*, R.L. Stevenson's *Dr Jekyll and Mr Hyde*, Edgar Allan Poe's *Ligeia*, Bulwer Lytton's *The Haunted and the Haunters*, etc. Too extreme an application of human will or thought creates a *destructive* situation, creates dangers, fears, terrors which can be countered only by correcting the original 'sin' of overreaching, of the mis-application of human knowledge or scientific procedure. This Frankenstein type of myth could be represented diagrammatically as:

Figure 1   *Source of metamorphosis or strangeness within the self*

where the circle of the self generates its own power for destruction and metamorphosis.

In the second kind of myth, fear originates in a source external to the subject: the self suffers an attack of some sort which makes it part of the other. This is the type of appropriation of the subject found in *Dracula* and tales of vampirism: it is a sequence of invasion, metamorphosis and fusion, in which an external force enters the subject, changes it irreversibly and usually gives to it the power to initiate similar transformations. Kafka's *Metamorphosis* is of this type, as are many films which have developed in a fantastic genre, such as George Romero's *Night of the Living Dead*. This could be seen as:

Figure 2   *Source of metamorphosis external to self*

with external forces entering the subject, effecting
metamorphosis and moving out again into the world.
Unlike the Frankenstein type, this Dracula type of myth is
not confined to the individual subject: it involves a whole
network of other beings and frequently has to draw upon a
mechanical reproduction of religious beliefs or magical
devices to contain the threat. In *Dracula*, there is a recourse
to Christian devices (the crucifix, the Bible) and to magic
(garlic, incantations) to defeat the fear of a complete invasion by vampiric figures, and in *Night of the Living Dead,* a
recourse to scientific explanation (radiation, which galvan-
ized the dead into the un-dead) and military/technological
power to destroy the half-living zombies activated by a
radiation leakage.

In the Frankenstein type of myth (of which Faust is a
variant), self becomes other through a self-generated
metamorphosis, through the subject's alienation from himself and consequent splitting or multiplying of identities
(structured around themes of the 'I'). In the Dracula type of
myth (of which Don Juan is a variant), otherness is established through a fusion of self with something outside, producing a new form, an 'other' reality (structured around
themes of the 'not-I'). This second type centralizes the problem of *power*: Dracula, like Romero's zombies, collects con-
quests, collects victims to prove the power of possession, to
try to establish a total, self-supporting system. Both the
Frankenstein and Dracula myths push towards a state of
undifferentiation of self from other. In the following sections, some psychoanalytic theories will be introduced in an
attempt to articulate some of the unconscious drives behind
these two mythical patterns which dominate and determine

the modern fantastic, but the second type, the Dracula myth, is far less easy to 'contain', far more disturbing in its countercultural thrust. It is not confined to *one* individual; it tries to replace cultural life with a total, absolute otherness, a completely alternative self-sustaining system.

# 3 PSYCHOANALYTICAL PERSPECTIVES

ONE of the major shortcomings of Todorov's book on the fantastic is its reluctance to engage with psychoanalytic theory and, related to this, a relative lack of attention to the broader ideological implications of fantastic literature. Ideology – roughly speaking, the imaginary ways in which men experience the real world, those ways in which men's relation to the world is lived through various systems of meaning such as religion, family, law, moral codes, education, culture, etc. – is not something simply handed down from one conscious mind to another, but is profoundly *unconscious*. It seems to me that it is important, when dealing with a kind of literature which deals so repeatedly with unconscious material, not to ignore the ways in which that material re-presents the relations between ideology and the human subject. Todorov adamantly rejects psychoanalytic readings, insisting that 'Psychosis and neurosis are not the explication of the themes of fantastic literature' (p.154). Yet his attention to themes of self and other, of 'I' and 'not-I', opens on to issues of interrelationship and of the determination of relations between human subjects by unconscious desire, issues which can only be understood by turning to psychoanalysis. As

Bellemin-Noël points out in his article which provides a critique of Todorov's position, it is a mistake to suppose that the only use of psychoanalysis would be to account for the content of fantasy. On the contrary, the problem is one of examining 'how the *formal* aspects of the fantastic are themselves in liaison with the workings and/or the configurations of the *unconscious discourse*' (Bellemin-Noël, p.117).

It is strange that Todorov evades this question, for his understanding of the modern fantastic points to it as emerging most strongly during the course of the nineteenth century, at precisely that juncture when readings of otherness as supernatural (his category of the 'marvellous') were being slowly replaced and disturbed by readings of otherness as natural and subjectively generated (his category of the 'uncanny'). It is in this period, as we have seen, that the demonic ceased to be a supernatural category and developed into a much more equivocal notion, suggesting that alienation, metamorphosis, doubling, transformation of the subject, were expressions of unconscious desire, and were not 'accounted for' as reflections or manifestations of supernatural or magical intervention. Indeed, as Bellemin-Noël writes, 'One could define fantastic literature as that in which the question of the unconscious emerges'.

The fantastic is a literature which attempts to create a space for a discourse other than a conscious one and it is this which leads to its problematization of language, of the word, in its utterance of desire. The formal and thematic features of fantastic literature are similarly determined by this (impossible) attempt to find a language for desire. By focussing so exclusively on the structural *effects* of the text, Todorov elides these issues. It is only by turning to psychoanalysis, considering some of the theoretical accounts of the structures of unconscious desire, that those narrative effects and forms can be seen as manifestations of deeper cultural issues, to do with the placing of the subject in a social context, in language. By working through Freud's theories of the uncanny towards his theories of the constitution of the human subject, it is possible to see the modern fantastic as a literature preoccupied with unconscious desire and to relate this desire to cultural order, thereby correcting Todorov's neglect of ideological issues.

## The uncanny

> With no stars to help him, his sense of orientation has become uncanny . . .
>
> Mervyn Peake, *Gormenghast*

> Nor could I ever after see the world as I had known it. Mixed with the present scene was always a little of the past and a little of the future, and every once-familiar object loomed alien in the new perspective brought on by my widened sight. From then on I walked in a fantastic dream of unknown and half-known shapes; and with each new gateway crossed, the less plainly could I recognize the things of the narrow sphere to which I had so long been bound.
>
> H.P. Lovecraft, *The Book*

The 'uncanny' is a term which has been used philosophically as well as in psychoanalytic writing, to indicate a disturbing, vacuous area. Heidegger described as 'uncanny' that empty space produced by a loss of faith in divine images. Unable to reach, or to imagine reaching, 'God's sphere of being', man is left with a sense of vacancy. 'Indeed,' writes Heidegger, 'in proportion with this impossibility [of setting himself in the place of God] something far more *uncanny* may happen . . . The place which, metaphysically speaking, belongs to God . . . can remain empty. Instead of it another, that is, a metaphysically corresponding place can appear, which is neither identical with God's sphere of being nor with that of man' (cit. Buber, p.91). The emergence of modern fantasy coincides with a recognition of this uncanny region. According to the *Oxford English Dictionary*, the earliest recorded use of the word 'uncanny' as meaning 'not quite safe to trust to' is in 1773. By 1785 it means 'dangerous, unsafe'. Jorge Louis Borges has identified its first fictional appearance as being William Beckford's strange oriental Gothic fantasy *Vathek* (1784): 'this adjective [uncanny] is applicable to certain pages of *Vathek*, and I can recall it in no other book before then' (Borges, p.191).

It is a term recurring time after time throughout nineteenth-century fantasy. Chamisso's *Peter Schlemihl* describes a disturbing meeting with a shadow or devil, 'no one seemed to consider the incident as at all extraordinary. To me all this was becoming increasingly *uncanny*, indeed quite horrifying.' [1] Bulwer Lytton's *Zanoni* claims 'the whole thing looked uncanny'.[2] Lewis Carroll's *Sylvie and Bruno* tells of its narrator's 'not unpleasant thrill' at an '*uncanny* coincidence' and a confused doubling of identities: 'I was more startled than I liked to show. There was something so *uncanny* in this echo.' [3] Bram Stoker's *Dracula* records Harker's apprehension of the vampire's castle: 'This was all so strange and uncanny that a dreadful fear came upon me', and Lucy's frightened laughter sounds 'a little uncanny'.[4] Later, there is Mary L. Pendered's *The Uncanny House* (1929). It is a term used both to describe and to create unease. (In French, the uncanny = 'l'inquiétante étrangeté'.)

Freud's seminal essay on the uncanny was first published in 1919.[5] It provides a clear theoretical introduction to psychoanalytic readings of fantastic literature, especially to nineteenth-century works, where the uncanny is at its most explicit. Freud begins with a fairly wide definition. 'The *uncanny* . . . is undoubtedly related to what is frightening – to what arouses dread and horror . . . it tends to coincide with what excites fear in general' (p.219). He proceeds to a more particular theory, reading the uncanny as the effect of projecting unconscious desires and fears into the environment and on to other people. Frightening scenes of uncanny literature are produced by hidden anxieties concealed within the subject, who then interprets the world in terms of his or her apprehensions. The uncanny constitutes 'that class of the frightening which leads back to what is known of old and long familiar'.

As Freud points out, there are two levels of meaning to the German term for the uncanny, *das Unheimlich*. Both levels are vital for an understanding of his theory in relation to fantasy. *Das Heimlich*, the un-negated version, is ambivalent. On the first level of meaning, it signifies that which is homely, familiar, friendly, cheerful, comfortable, intimate. It gives a sense of being 'at home' in the world, and its negation therefore summons up the unfamiliar, uncomfortable, strange, alien. It produces a feeling of estrangement, of being not 'at home' in the world. The few examples of the uncanny quoted above all have this effect. A second level of meaning begins to explain the uncanny's disturbing powers. *Das Heimlich* also means that which is concealed from others: all that is hidden, secreted, obscured. Its negation, *das Unheimlich*, then functions to dis-cover, reveal, expose areas normally kept out of sight. The uncanny combines these two semantic levels: its signification lies precisely in this dualism. It uncovers what is hidden and, by doing so, effects a disturbing transformation of the familiar into the unfamiliar.

Fantastic literature transforms the 'real' through this kind of dis-covery. It does not introduce novelty, so much as uncover all that needs to remain hidden if the world is to be comfortably 'known'. Its uncanny effects reveal an obscure, occluded region which lies behind the homely (*heimlich*) and native (*heimisch*). As the term 'paraxis' has already suggested, fantasy lies alongside the axis of the real, and many of the prepositional constructions which are used to introduce a fantastic realm emphasize its interstitial placing. 'On the edge', 'through', 'beyond', 'between', 'at the back of', 'underneath', or adjectives such as 'topsy-turvy', 'reversed', 'inverted'. This area, according to Freud, is one of concealed desire. 'Something has to be added to what is novel and unfamiliar', he claims, 'to make it uncanny (. . .) it is in reality nothing new or alien, but something which is familiar and old – established in the mind and become alienated from it only through the process of repression.' What is encountered in this uncanny realm, whether it is termed spirit, angel, devil, ghost, or monster, is nothing but an unconscious *projection*, projections being those 'qualities, feelings, wishes, objects, which the subject refuses to recognize or rejects in himself [and which] are expelled from the self and located in another person or thing' (Laplanche and Pontalis, p.349).

Otto Rank's *Idea of the Holy* (1917) reads *das Unheimlich* as a continued expression of man's need to locate fear in unnatural figures. Through secularization, a religious sense of the numinous is transformed and reappears as a sense of the uncanny, but the psychological origins of both are identical. Rank interprets 'demons' and 'gods' as produced from this same root of unconscious fear, and 'all the products of "mythological apperception" or "fantasy" ' as 'nothing but different modes in which it has been objectified' (cit. Prawer, p.15). Literary fantasies, then, have a function corresponding to the mythical and magical products of other cultures. They return us to what Freud identifies as an animistic mode of perception, that thought process which characterizes primitive man at an evolutionary stage prior to his concession to a 'reality principle'. Freud writes that we 'attribute an "uncanny" quality to impressions that seek to confirm the omnipotence of thoughts and the animistic mode of thinking in general' (*Totem and Taboo*, p.86).

Freud's paradigm of the uncanny in literature is E.T.A. Hoffmann's 'fantastic narrative' *The Sandman* (1816–17). Nathaniel, the tale's hero, cannot separate real from apparently unreal events. He confuses a figure of a sandman with his father's lawyer, Coppelius, then with an Italian optician, Coppola. This confusion derives from *taking literally* a metaphor (cf. Donne's 'I *am* every dead thing') of the sandman as 'a wicked man who comes when children won't go to bed, and throws handfuls of sand in their eyes so that they jump out of their heads all bleeding.' [6] Nathaniel falls in love with Olympia, who seems real, but is a doll. Less and less able to understand or discriminate between 'seems' and 'is' (the two become one), he tries to murder his sister, Clara, at the top of a tower (thinking she is 'the wooden doll') but stops when he perceives Coppelius (the sandman) below and he leaps to his death. Freud identifies various uncanny features in the tale, particularly a compulsive behaviour pattern, a doubling and multiplying of characters, an animation of inanimate objects. All of these, writes Freud, are produced by Nathaniel's unconscious fears. What is experienced as uncanny is an objectification of the subject's anxieties, read into shapes external to himself.

At the centre of Freud's analysis of *The Sandman* is his interpretation of Nathaniel's phobia about 'eyes' (he fears Coppelius-Coppola because of their unconscious association with the sandman) as revealing a deep-seated terror which constitutes 'a castration complex' – a fear that paternal threats to punish the boy's sexual activities would be realized. Psychoanalytic readings of this kind can be applied to various fantastic narratives: stories by Poe, Dostoevsky, James, have been analysed as fantastic projections generated from the subject's unconscious desire.[7] But Hélène Cixous has written a critique of Freud's essay which reveals some of its omissions. She points out that Freud's exclusive focus on the motif of eyes permits him to elide the other central uncanny feature, the doll which comes to life, and to overlook what her animation might signify. Cixous sees Freud as 'jumping from one effect to another until he reaches the "point of certainty", or reality, which he wishes to present as a solid rock upon which he can base his analytic argument' (p.205). By placing himself in a position of rational confidence towards the tale, Freud imposes upon it a positive unity: he closes its 'open' structure. Cixous moves beyond this positivism in her approach to the uncanny. Her understanding of its *relationality* corresponds to and begins to account for a theory of fantasy as defined by its relation to the 'real', thus linking its thematic and formal qualities, for both dissolve closed structures.

The uncanny, writes Cixous, exists only in relation to the familiar and the normal. It is tangential, to one side. It 'only presents itself, initially, on the edge of something else'. Defined by its relationality, it subverts any re-presentation of a unified reality. It is 'a relational signifier . . . for the uncanny is in effect *composite*, it infiltrates itself in between things, in the interstices, it asserts a *gap* where one would like to be assured of unity' (p.208). Her structural understanding of the uncanny as *a mode of apprehending* links fantasy to grotesque art: 'The grotesque is a structure . . . it is the estranged world, our world which has been transformed' (Kayser, p.184). The uncanny, however, removes structure. It empties the 'real' of its 'meaning', it leaves signs without significance. Cixous presents its unfamiliarity not as merely displaced sexual anxiety, but as a rehearsal of an encounter with death, which is pure absence. Death cannot be portrayed directly: it appears in literature either as figura (emblem) such as the medieval *memento mori* skeletons, or as mere space. This is materialized as a ghost: 'the immediate figure of strangeness is the ghost. The ghost is the fiction of our relation to death made concrete.' *Das Unheimlich* is at its purest here, where we dis-cover our latent deaths, our hidden lack of being, for 'nothing is both better known and stranger to thought than mortality . . . "Death" has no shape in life. Our unconscious has no room for a representation of our mortality' (p.213).

Ghost stories are a special category of the fantastic, evolving from folklore and developing through Gothic horror fiction to become widely popularized in the Victorian period, through the works of Sheridan Le Fanu, M.R. James, Rudyard Kipling, Arthur Machen, Vernon Lee, Henry James, etc. Although the very term 'ghost' suggests a sliding towards the supernatural and the marvellous, away from more material and ambiguous 'unrealities' of the fantastic, the effect of ghost tales is similarly disturbing, for they imply the return of the dead as the undead. They disrupt the crucial defining line which separates 'real' life from the 'unreality' of death, subverting those discrete units by which unitary meaning or 'reality' is constituted. Gillian Beer describes the ghost story as a form eliding 'the distance between the actual and the imagined' so that 'frail and cherished distinctions collapse'. In the place of these discriminations appears a space, an absence of difference:

> [With the ghost story] the fictional *takes place* in the everyday: it takes space, and it is this usurpation of space by the immaterial which is one of the deepest terrors released by the ghost story . . . Ghost stories are to do with the insurrection, not the resurrection of the dead.[8]

By attempting to make visible that which is culturally invisible and which is written out as negation and as death, the fantastic introduces absences. Hence the tendency of fantasy towards non-signification. There can be no adequate linguistic representation of this 'other', for it has no place in life, and it is this contradiction which gives rise to the disjunction between signifier and signified which is at the centre of the fantastic. Fantasy's re-placing of presence by absence attempts to introduce this non-signifying area, this 'thing' called death, which Cixous terms 'signifier without signified . . . absolute secret, absolute newness, which should stay hidden, for if it is manifested to me, it means I am dead: only the dead know the secret of death' (p.231). The cultural, or countercultural, implications of this assertion of non-signification are far-reaching, for it represents a dissolution of a culture's signifying practice, the very means by which it establishes meaning.

Un-doing those unifying structures and significations upon which social order depends, fantasy functions to subvert and undermine cultural stability. It proposes what Cixous calls 'a subtle invitation to transgression' by exposing the relative and arbitrary nature of those 'responses [which men make] to death: ideological institutions, religion, politics'.

As a literature of absences, fantasy throws back on to the dominant culture a constant reminder of something 'other', thereby 'indicating the vanity of notions of limit and discrimination . . . making that vanity its subject' (Bessière, p.63). It is opposed to institutional order. Freud is well aware of the countercultural effects of a literature of the uncanny, and its transgressive function in bringing to light things which should remain obscure. The uncanny *expresses* drives which have to be *repressed* for the sake of cultural continuity. Freud regards anything uncanny, or anything provoking dread, as being subject to cultural taboo. A resurfacing of long familiar anxieties/desires in uncanny incidents constitutes 'a return of the repressed'.

Freud's *Totem and Taboo* (1912–13) provides a theoretical background to this pattern of repression. Taboos are the strongest inhibitions which a culture imposes to guarantee its survival. The major ones, according to Freud, are taboos on incest (a desire for the mother) and death (a desire to touch or make contact with corpses). There are many literary fantasies of violating these taboos by telling of incest, necrophilia, ghosts, vampires, the un-dead. Incest fantasies of the Romantic period, for example, include Walpole's *The Mysterious Mother*, Tieck's *Der blonde Eckbert*, Schiller's *Die Braut von Messina*, Grillparzer's *Die Ahnfrau*, Chateaubriand's *René*, leading to Melville's *Pierre, or the Ambiguities*, and Poe's *The Fall of the House of Usher*. On this level, fantasies make up for a society's prohibitions by allowing vicarious fulfilment. Fantasies express libidinal drives towards satisfaction, the libido being that part of the self (according to Freud) which struggles against submitting to the reality principle. As the locus of absolute desire, the libido seeks absolute satisfaction, refusing to acknowledge 'realistic' restraints.

Freud links the uncanny to an animistic mode of perception which defies the reality principle. He identifies this mode on both a phylogenetic (cultural) and ontogenetic (individual) level, in terms of man's evolution towards a human 'reality'. Both levels involve a gradual renunciation of animistic thinking (and libidinal desire) as this evolutionary process advances. Both effect a slow movement away from a fantasy world towards external necessity, or *Ananke*. There are three crucial stages of this development which can be summarized, from Freud's writings, as follows:

| *Phylogenetic evolution* | *Ontogenetic evolution* |
|---|---|
| 1  ANIMISTIC<br>Men ascribe omnipotence<br>to themselves. | NARCISSISM/<br>AUTO-EROTICISM |
| 2  RELIGIOUS<br>Power is transferred to gods, yet<br>the individual believes he has<br>some influence with them. | ATTACHMENT TO<br>LOVE OBJECTS |
| 3  SCIENTIFIC<br>Leaves no room for human omni-<br>potence. The subject becomes<br>resigned to the laws of necessity,<br>and the inevitability of death. | ABANDONMENT<br>TO REALITY<br>PRINCIPLE |

A child's growth from a narcissistic stage of self-love to a reality principle corresponds, on an individual level, to the movement of man's cultural history from a magical to a scientific world view. Both narcissism and animism permit a belief in the omnipotence of thought and in 'all the other creations with the help of which man, in the unrestricted narcissism of that stage of development, strives to fend off the manifest prohibitions of reality . . . everything that now strikes us as "uncanny" fulfils the condition of touching these residues of animistic mental activity within us and bringing them to expression' (Freud, 'The uncanny', p.240).

Freud's tripartite scheme is useful for considering some of the conflicts narrated through fantasies of narcissism and dualism, and it will be reintroduced in discussing images of disintegration and dismemberment. A literature of the uncanny, by permitting an articulation of taboo subjects which are otherwise silenced, threatens to transgress social norms. Fantasies are not, however, countercultural merely through this thematic transgression. On the contrary, they frequently serve (as does Gothic fiction) to re-confirm institutional order by supplying a vicarious fulfilment of desire and neutralizing an urge towards transgression. A more subtle and subversive use of the fantastic appears with works which threaten to disrupt or eat away at the 'syntax' or *structure* by which order is made. The following section will discuss some of the unconscious drives behind this erosive activity.

## Metamorphosis and entropy

> . . . the most awful, most secret forces . . . lie at the heart of all things . . . a presence, that was neither man nor beast, neither the living nor the dead, but all things mingled, the form of all things but devoid of all form.
>
> Arthur Machen, *The Great God Pan* (1894)

The fantastic can be seen as corresponding to the first stage in Freud's evolutionary model, that stage of a magical and animistic thought mode when primitive man and the young child have no sense of difference between self and other, subject and object worlds. Fantasy, with its tendency to dissolve structures, moves towards an ideal of *undifferentiation*, and this is one of its defining characteristics. It refuses difference, distinction, homogeneity, reduction, discrete forms. This desire for undifferentiation is close to the instinct which Freud identified in *Beyond the Pleasure Principle* (1920), and in his late works, as the most fundamental drive in man: a drive towards a state of inorganicism. This has been crudely termed 'a death wish', but it is not a simple desire to cease to be. Freud sees it as the most radical form of the pleasure principle, a longing for Nirvana, where all tensions are reduced. This condition he termed a state of *entropy*, and the desire for undifferentiation he termed an *entropic* pull, opposing entropy to energy, to the erotic, aggressive drives of any organism.

Modern fantasy makes explicit this attraction towards an entropic state. It is, perhaps, at its most extreme in the violent writings of Sade, whose fantasies anticipate much subsequent fiction in their pull towards a zero point, a condition of entropy. Sade's ideal is an absolute blurring of identities, a promiscuity (i.e. a mixed, disordered, indiscriminate, heterogeneous dis-unity). One of Sade's innumerable libertines, for example, longs for a combination of species, where gender and genre would cease to be separating categories.

> I have discovered that when it is a question of someone like me, born for libertinage, it is useless to think of imposing limits or restraints upon oneself – impetuous desires immediately sweep them away. In a word, my dear, I am an amphibious creature: I love everything, everyone, whatever it is, it amuses me. I should like to combine every species.[9]

Sade urges transgression of the limits separating self from other, man from woman, human from animal, organic from inorganic objects. He seeks a defiant and violent disorder, a fluidity, a lack of discretion.

Instead of a separation into discrete selves, Sade proposes 'a universal prostitution of all beings', providing unity with nature in a state of perpetual motion. Death, he suggests, ceases to signify: it is merely a translation of forms, a kind of metamorphosis. The transition from life to death then ceases to terrify, or to give 'life' any dignity or supremacy over 'death' – Sade refuses to give to the first a positive and to the second a negative categorization. 'Dissolution', he writes, 'is a very great state of motion.' Nothingness ('death') is no less present than live matter:

There is no moment when the body of the animal is at rest; it never dies; but because it no longer exists for us, we believe that it no longer exists at all. Bodies are transmuted . . . metamorphosed, but they are never inert. Inertia is absolutely impossible for matter whether matter is organized or not. Weigh these truths carefully and you will see where they lead and what a twist they give to human morality.[10]

Sade's materialistic atheism substitutes nature in a state of perpetual motion for God. Social order, ethics, morality, institutionalized activity, are all revealed as 'un-natural' constructs imposed upon a natural disorder, to which Sade attempts to return. He seeks to un-do differentiating cultural structures and to betray their vanity, their relativity. 'Nothingness', he writes, 'has never held terrors for me, in it I see naught but what is consoling and unpretentious; all the other theories are of pride's composition, this alone is of reason's.'[11]

The consequence of this embrace of natural disorder and of utter disregard for social difference is that Sade's fantasies are the most extreme articulations of a desire for transgression in our cultural history. *120 Days of Sodom* (1785), *Justine, or the Misfortunes of Virtue* (1791), *Eugénie de Franval*, and *Juliette* have been acknowledged as the most transgressive of all literary fantasies. Bataille calls *120 Days of Sodom* 'the book that can be said to dominate all books' for its utterance of 'the true fury which man holds within him' (Bataille, *Literature and Evil*, p.88). Maurice Blanchot claims *Justine* as the most scandalous of all texts, 'we can admit that there has never been such an outrageous work in the literature of any other age . . . none other has so offended human feelings and thoughts . . . it is the most scandalous work ever written . . . an undeniable absolute' (Blanchot, *Lautréamont et Sade*, p.17).

Sade's utterance of desire breaks every cultural taboo. His representations of acts of incest transgress family law; representations of sodomy transgress 'natural' laws of sexuality as reproductive; murder, torture, necrophilia, transgress laws against intercourse with the dead. And by indicating the bisexuality of desire (refusing distinctions between male and female gender), Sade questions the sexed identity of the subject, anticipating explorations of sexual difference through thematic clusters in the fantastic, such as metamorphosis, vampirism, androgyny, etc. Yet Sade's texts are as important on a *syntactic* level as on a *semantic* one. It is not only the themes of transgression which make his work subversive, but the means of their representation. His fantasies are long, apparently interminable, for the semantics of desire are never exhausted by the particular combinations in which they are articulated. Sade termed his works 'strange fantasies which double the effect of desire, without extinguishing it'. If they reached the end of their desire, they would cease to be, for *desire* cannot exist without lack, without a gap between satisfaction sought and satisfaction obtained. Sade's attempt to sustain his fantasies whilst closing this gap creates a vertiginous effect of language erasing itself in its impossible realization of desire.

The impossible quest for a 'language' for desire consists, in Sade's work, of pushing ordinary discourse to its limits, to the point of rupture. Damisch writes that 'Sade set up *another* language: a language where the limits of humanist discourse are broken . . . a word which expresses the other side of life.' [12] Bataille has commented similarly, claiming that Sade's fantasies give 'a rational expression to those uncontrollable desires, on the negation of which consciousness has based the social structures and the very image of man. It was in order to do this that he had to question every value which had hitherto been considered absolute . . . by an exasperated inversion, he wanted the impossible and the *reverse* of life . . .' (Bataille, p.98).

Irène Bessière situates this problem of fantasy's language of desire in relation to Sartre's philosophical distinctions between the *thetic* and the *non-thetic*. Whereas the thetic signifies propositions (theses) which are taken to be real, rational, and substantial, the non-thetic suggests their opposite, an unreality. The non-thetic, by definition, can have no adequate linguistic form, for it exists before, or outside, human language. Since fantastic narrative relies upon words for its being, it cannot belong to the non-thetic – if it did, it would cease to be. It does, however, attempt to belong to it. It is situated *between* the thetic and the non-thetic, positioned within the first and pushing (back) towards the second. Sade's fantasies do not actually *break* syntactic structures: they push syntax to its limits, eroding, yet sustaining it. The thetic remains undisturbed, so that a transgressive thrust is all the more vertiginous. The writing of Blanchot and Bataille in many ways belongs to this literature of transgression, dissolving forms *within* the thetic.

Sade's writing can be seen as an extreme point, towards which other modern fantasies move and against which they can be located. For Sade uses language to eradicate itself, not to *transcend* the verbal, but to rupture and violate it in a desire for something which, through language, has been distanced. This tendency towards violence and rupture can be related to Sade's equally aggressive atheism, which prevents a desire for otherness from taking the form of transcendence on to a different plane. He adamantly rejects the concept of divinity, insisting that 'Things necessarily come about without being determined by a superior intelligence ... It is possible that everything derives logically from a primary cause, without there being reason or wisdom in that primary cause ... natural causes sufficing, there is no need to invent such unnatural ones as your god ... 'tis plain your god is superfluous, he is perfectly useless ... imaginary only, null and therefore non-existent.' [13] The 'idea of God' is a 'fault in man' that Sade can neither forgive nor tolerate.

Informing Sade's repudiation of humanistic and Christian ideals, then, is a fundamental desire to push the 'human' beyond itself, without having recourse to fictions of supernaturalism or of divinity. His goal is the same as that goal which lies behind all fantastic art, to a greater or lesser degree, the arrival at a point of absolute unity of self and other, subject and object, at a zero point of entropy. Jacques Lacan has identified the longing for this unity as the profoundest desire of the subject, referring to it as 'an eternal and irreducible human desire . . . an eternal desire for the nonrelationship of zero, where identity is meaningless' (*The Language of the Self*, p.191).

Such a haunting longing for absolute identity of self and other reappears in violent form in Lautréamont's *Maldoror* (1868), perhaps the fantasy closest to Sade's extreme. Maldoror's desire to be ever-changing in form has been described by Bersani as seeking 'to become everything without ever losing the self: a permanent metamorphosis without change' (p.221); and Blanchot has recognized it as 'la hantise du semblable', the longing for self as other, for symbiosis. Maldoror celebrates his body's interchangeability with animal life and with inorganic matter. He has lived 'a half-century in the form of a shark', has been both swan and pig: 'A man, a stone, or a tree', he chants, 'is going to begin this fourth song.' Human, bird, beast and amphibian forms merge together in an assertion of instability, of 'this ambiguous plurality in myself'. Nothing is stable or unitary: the subject is multiple, metamorphic.

> I saw a human being swimming in the sea, with the large webbed feet of a duck instead of arms and legs and a dorsal fin proportionately as long and streamlined as a dolphin's, strong of muscle, and followed by numerous shoals of fish . . . let it be known that man, by his multiple and complex nature, is not unaware of the means of extending its frontiers . . .[14]

Lautréamont's Maldoror, like Sade's libertines, longs for absolute otherness, yet refuses to believe in the existence of any divine being. God, when made visible, is parodic and grotesque, linked with death and with waste. 'Not finding what I was seeking, I lifted my eyes higher, and higher still, until I saw a throne made of human excrement and gold, on which was sitting – with idiotic pride, his body draped in a shroud of unwashed hospital linen – he who calls himself the Creator!' (p.85). Maldoror's 'insatiable thirst for the infinite' cannot be satisfied by this old phantom and the subject turns instead to natural zero points. His ideal is the sea, where everything is fluid, unseparated, without distinction: 'Old ocean, you are the symbol of identity: always equal to yourself.' And this ideal can never be realized without rupture or transformation of the 'human' body, for the identity of that body imposes restriction and constraints. 'I cannot, cannot satisfy this need', laments Maldoror, 'I am the son of a man and a woman . . . This astonishes me . . . I believed I was something more' (p.39).

This frustration and violent rupture in Sade and in Lautréamont points to a marked contrast between their atheistic, secular fantasies and fantasies of a more religious nature. Their desire for 'a nonrelationship of zero, where identity is meaningless' is analogous to a mystical quest for union with an absolute 'Other'. But whereas a religious subject has faith that a sense of unbeing, a dissolution of the ego, will lead to ultimate unity with a divine beloved, a sceptical, atheistic subject has no such faith. In the place of transcendent ideals, there is discovered a zero point, a space of non-being, an absence.

The transgressive thrust of the modern fantastic points to a similarity between religious and secular fantasies, but with different effects. Both are concerned with *limits* and with the projected dissolution of these limits around the 'human', but one form slides from the human to the superhuman, whilst the other negates and inverts the human from within. Fantastic narrative is preoccupied with *limits*, and Michel Foucault's writings enable us to place this concern historically. In an essay on transgression in the work of Georges Bataille, Foucault compares the kind of transgressive literature found in secularized fantasy to religion in previous ages. He claims for them both the same ontological function: an exploration of the limits of being. Foucault suggests that a literature of transgression occupies the 'place where the sacred used to play, for transgression takes limit to the edge of its being, to the point where it virtually disappears, in a movement of pure violence'. He continues:

> Perhaps the emergence of sexuality in our culture is an event which has several levels of meaning: it is linked to the death of God and to that ontological void which that death left at the limits of our thought: it is also linked to something which is still obscure and tentative – a form of thinking in which an interrogation of *limits* replaces a search for totality and in which a movement of transgression replaces a movement of contradictions. It is linked, finally, to a questioning of language by itself, in a circularity which the 'outrageous' violence of erotic literature, far from breaking, manifests from its earliest entrance into language. (Foucault, 'Préface à la transgression', p.767)

Social and sexual transgression, the violent breaking of taboos in modern fantasy from Sade and Gothic fiction onwards, rejects limits imposed upon the 'human', yet the activity is one which is self-consuming, attacking nothing but the human, for without God, transgression is empty, a kind of profanation without an object.

The modern fantastic reveals itself to be less and less able to assume a transcendental role or to invent superworlds. It continues to articulate absolute desire, but its ends are no longer known: breaking finite, human limits, becomes its only (im)possibility. Moving towards an imaginary zero condition, without time or space, a condition of entropy, the fantastic produces an 'other' region, one which Maurice Blanchot's *Le pas au-delà* describes as the result of pure transgression: 'Transgression belongs neither to day nor to night . . . No before, no during, no afterwards. It is as if it were another region, a place different from all places' (cit. Arnaud, p.105). Ann Quin's recent fantasy, *Berg* (1977), represents this region as 'that space within, separated from life, as well as death', where 'there is no separation' of objects, 'only a distasteful similarity', no chronology, but a timelessness 'when eternity lies here inside, no division whatsoever, simply a series of circular motivations.' [15]

Freud insists that this pull towards a zero point is not a simple death wish. The pull towards entropy signifies the tendency of an organism to move towards stability, where the organic merges with the inorganic and where separate units fuse together. The subject is drawn back through the primitivism of the child, where 'everything is connected with everything else (so that) nothing is connected with anything else' (Piaget, p.61). Freud terms this condition of polymorphous disorder 'the quiescence of the inorganic world'.[16] Movement and stillness, life and death, subject and object, mind and matter, become as one. The impossibilities upon which fantastic narratives are structured (they have been defined as antinomical, oxymoronic in structure) can be related to this drive towards a realization of contradictory elements merging together in the desire for undifferentiation.

Edgar Allan Poe's fantasies and science fictions describe the zero point behind successive transformations of the subject as peculiarly full *and* empty, dynamic *and* static: it 'resembles death . . . it resembles the ultimate life; for I perceive things directly [as in] the ultimate unorganized life.' [17] His essay 'Mesmeric revelation' refers to organic, rudimentary creatures which 'enjoy the ultimate life – immortality – at death, or metamorphosis.' His desire is for 'that which *was not* . . . that which had no form . . . that which had no thought . . . all this nothingness . . . all this immortality.' [18] *The House of Usher* describes Usher's ideal as 'the kingdom of *inorganization*', and Poe's science fiction develops this ideal of natural unity, where everything is swallowed up, where 'Space and Duration are one . . . neither Past nor Future . . . all being Now.' (*Eureka*)

Many fantasies exhibit a kind of homeostasis, which realizes this zero condition, yet eventually tends to run down as the narrative proceeds – Peake's *Gormenghast* trilogy is one example of this. Sade's fantasies are the most resistant to this tendency to run down.

From the basic pull towards entropy derive many of the thematic clusters of the fantastic, from obsessions with death, cannibalism, animism, to graphic depictions of changes of form. Metamorphosis, with its stress upon instability of natural forms, obviously plays a large part in fantastic literature for this reason. Men transforming into women, children changing into birds or beasts, animals interchanging with plants, rocks, trees, stones, magical shifts of shape, size or colour, have constituted one of the primary pleasures of the fantasy mode. Yet there are some significant shifts in the use of metamorphosis. Fairy tales, allegories, medieval romance situate metamorphosis within a frame which gives it a teleological function. It serves either as a vehicle of meaning within the narrative, as concept, or metaphor, or symbol of redemption. Ovid's *Metamorphoses* records Daphne's famous transformation from woman to tree, but the change is effected through divine intercession, fulfilling Daphne's desire to be free from her female body.

> Her prayer was scarcely ended when a deep languor took hold on her limbs, her soft breast was enclosed in thin bark, her hair grew into leaves, her arms into branches, and her feet that were lately so swift were held fast by sluggish roots, while her face became the treetop. Nothing of her was left, except her shining loveliness.[19]

There are no delightful transformations of this kind from post-Romantic fantasy (as opposed to faery): changes are without meaning and are progressively without the will or desire of the subject. As with Kafka's *Metamorphosis*, physical transformations simply happen.

Irving Massey's *The Gaping Pig: Literature and Metamorphosis* (1976) provides a critical study of horrific versions of transformation throughout various fantasies. Apuleius's *The Golden Ass*, Gogol's *The Nose*, Carroll's *Alice in Wonderland*

and *Through the Looking-Glass*, Mary Shelley's *Frankenstein*, Prosper Merimée's *Lokis* and *Vénus d'Ille*, R.L. Stevenson's *Dr Jekyll and Mr Hyde*, and Bram Stoker's *Dracula* have the same desire to lose a separative human consciousness, and Massey regards this desire as having had only a grotesque fulfilment in fantastic literature.

Massey's arguments reinforce the point made earlier, that the fantastic is *not* metaphorical. It does not create images which are 'poetic', rather it produces a sliding of one form into another, in a metonymical displacement. This process is one which Massey identifies as metamorphic and 'it may be', he writes, 'that pleasure produces metaphor and fear metamorphosis . . . (for) in fear the *object* attains full reality' (p.218). Matter, the object, consumes the subject, and 'self' is lost. Metamorphosis is 'typically violent and flies in the face of reason. It does not lend itself to assimilation into pleasurable or consoling schemes . . . it has something typically ugly, monstrous, unabsorbable about it' (p.17). Like the gaping pig, fixed in an image of inaudible squealing, the fantastic object does not signify. Metamorphosis in the modern fantastic suggests that the slipping of object into subject is no longer redemptive and that 'perverse' images of mutilation/horror/monstrosity have taken precedence over utopian dreams of superhuman or magical transformations of the subject.

## Disintegrated bodies

> The sign of desire's dominance is the end of unity and totality, and the transformation of the portrait into several portraits at once partial and mobile.
>
> Leo Bersani, *A Future for Astyanax*

The many partial, dual, multiple and dismembered selves scattered throughout literary fantasies violate the most cherished of all human unities: the unity of 'character'. It is the power of the fantastic to interrogate the category of character – that definition of the self as a coherent, indivisible and continuous whole which has dominated Western thought for centuries and is celebrated in classic theatre and 'realistic' art alike. A reluctance to admit of the possible existence of partial or contradictory aspects of the self dominated literary practice in representing individual 'characters' throughout the eighteenth and nineteenth centuries. Typical of this position is the voice of Thomas Reid, an eminent commonsense philosopher who articulated this generally accepted concept of 'self' as a closed, unified structure. 'A part of a person', he writes, 'is a manifest absurdity. A person is something indivisible, and is what Leibniz calls a *monad*. My personal identity . . . implies the continued existence of the indivisible thing which I call myself' (Reid, pp.340–1).

Fantasies provide very different images of identity from the solid bodies found in 'realistic' fiction, different from the full-blooded, three-dimensional 'rounded' characters of George Eliot's *Middlemarch*, or Leo Tolstoy's *War and Peace*. Fantastic narratives are littered with far less substantial bodies, with unstable forms, whose identities are never definitively established. Yet it would be insufficient simply to recognize the existence of these fragmented selves and to read them as recurrent 'thematic' devices of fantastic art, as Louis Vax and other critics do. It is important to understand the radical consequences of an attack upon unified 'character', for it is precisely this subversion of unities of 'self' which constitutes the most radical transgressive function of the fantastic.

'Character' is itself an ideological concept, produced in the name of a 'realistic' representation of an actual, empirically verifiable reality outside the literary text. Realism, as an artistic practice, confirms the dominant ideas of what constitutes this outside reality, by pulling it into place, organizing and framing it through the unities of the text. It presents its practice as a neutral, innocent and natural one, erasing its own artifice and *construction* of the 'real'. 'Character' is one of the central pivots of this operation. As Hélène Cixous writes:

The ideology underlying this fetishization of 'character' is that of an 'I' who is a *whole* subject, conscious, knowable; and the enunciatory 'I' *expresses himself* in the text, just as the world is *represented* complementarily in the text in a form equivalent to pictorial representation, as a simulacrum. So long as we do not put aside 'character' and everything it implies in terms of illusion and complicity with classical reasoning and the appropriating economy that such reasoning supports, we will remain locked up in the treadmill of reproduction. ('The character of "character" ', pp.305, 307)

The fantastic problematizes representation of the 'real', be it in terms of linguistic competence, or of fabricating monistic versions of 'real' time, space, or character. Increasingly, in post-Romantic literature, the fantastic draws attention to difficulties of representation and to conventions of literary discourse. By foregrounding its own signifying practice, the fantastic begins to betray its version of the 'real' as a relative one, which can only deform and transform experience, so the 'real' is exposed as a category, as something articulated by and constructed through the literary or artistic text. As Rabkin notes, the fantastic takes words and can 'reconfigure their semantic range [by putting them] in new contexts' (Rabkin, p.26).

By presenting discrete elements which are juxtaposed and then reassembled in unexpected, apparently impossible combinations, fantastic art draws explicit attention to the *process* of representation. It moves towards an 'anarchic discourse' by combining units in new relations, rather like Lautréamont's impossible juxtapositions in *Maldoror* (taken by André Breton as a classic instance of surrealistic method): 'Beautiful like the chance meeting of an umbrella and a sewing machine on an operating table'. Again, though, it should be stressed that the fantastic does not proceed by analogy – it is not based upon simile and comparison (like, as, as if) but upon equation (this *did* happen). With the problem of 'character', the fantastic does not introduce scenes *as if* they were real (except when it moves into allegory, dream vision, or the marvellous): it insists upon the *actuality* of the transformation (as in *Jekyll and Hyde* or in Kafka's *Metamorphosis*).

It is not difficult to find examples of radically dismembered selves in fantastic art. From the paintings of Hieronymus Bosch through a grotesque 'tradition' of visual and verbal fantasies, to Max Ernst, Salvador Dali, Jacques Prévert, André Breton, persons in the fantastic are imaged as scattered objects, dislocated and distanced from themselves. Rimbaud's famous declaration of non-coincidence with himself, 'Je est un autre',[20] anticipates Artaud's and Chaikin's violently disintegrated subjects.[21] Magnification, diminution, re-construction of various parts of the self are common in allegorical and satirical fantasy, as they relativize perception or introduce a brave new world. The purely fantastic, however, has little purposive transformation. Changes *are*, without meaning. There is no overall teleological scheme to give the transformation a meaning. Beasts, insects, shadows, monsters, are all 'self', from Gotthelf's *Black Spider* (1842) to Stoker's *Dracula* and Hans Ewers's *The Spider*.

Lewis Carroll's Alice suffers shrinkage, elongation, virtual disappearance, but this metamorphosis does not modify her sensibility. Maupassant's *The Hand*, Gogol's *The Nose*, Philip Roth's *The Breast* (re-working a repulsive scene from *Gulliver's Travels* and taking literally its metaphor of a giant mammary gland so that here the narrator *is* the breast) tell of parts of bodies with lives of their own, but signifying nothing. Roald Dahl's story *William and Mary* gives disturbing immortality to an eye, which replaces, or is, the 'he' of which it was once only an attribute: 'It grew bigger and bigger and in the end it was the only thing that she could see – a sort of face in itself.' [22] This kind of substitution of name for thing, or of part of a thing for the whole, opens up possibilities for a linguistic study of fantasy as working through metonymic and synecdochic processes of elision and substitution, as well as reinforcing the argument by Mark Nash as to the centrality of a play upon pronoun functions in the fantastic.

'Character' dispersal and fragmentation are the subject of much literature from the late eighteenth century onwards, both inside and outside fiction. Accumulated evidence, found in Ellenberger's massive study *The History of the Unconscious* and in Hunter and Macalpine's documentation of texts, *Three Hundred Years of Psychiatry*, indicates a gradual erosion of ideas of psychic unity over the last two centuries. Long before Freud, monistic definitions of self were being supplanted by hypotheses of dipsychism (dual selves) and polypsychism (multiple selves). 'A terrible idea came to me: "Man is double", I said to myself . . . In every man there is a spectator and an actor, one who speaks and one who replies . . . In all events, the *other* is hostile to me . . .' [23] Any individual is 'capable of various psychical states, with varying degrees of consciousness'.[24] George MacDonald's *Lilith* is only one amongst many Victorian voices which apprehended a polypsychic identity as a lack of self:

> I became at once aware that I could give him no notion of who I was. Indeed, who was I? . . . Then I understood that I did not know myself, did not know what I was, had no grounds on which to determine that I was one and not another. As for the name I went by in my own world, I had forgotten it, and did not care to recall it, for it meant nothing, and what it might be was plainly of no consequence here.[25]

Traditional literary criticism tends to read this fragmentation of character as a popular 'theme' of post-Romantic texts, or as a 'symbol' of divided consciousness, and conscience. Studies of the motif of the double encourage allegorical readings of otherness as 'evil'. Psychoanalytic works on literary doubles, however, by Otto Rank, Rogers, Keppler, have indicated possible Freudian readings of fragmented selves. 'Fantastic' character deformation suggests a radical refusal of the structures, the 'syntax' of cultural order. Incoherent, fluid selves exist in opposition to precious portraits of individuals as whole or essential. They break the boundaries separating self from other, leaving structures dissolved, or ruptured, through a radical open-endedness of being. The fantastic makes an assault upon the 'sign' of unified character and this has far-reaching consequences in terms of interrogating the process of character construction.

One of the most exciting critical studies of the breakdown of realistic unity in character presentation is Leo Bersani's *A Future for Astyanax: Character and Desire in Literature* (1975). Bersani employs the word 'desire' in a way which deliberately blurs its conceptual boundaries. He means it to gesture towards 'an area of human projection going beyond the limits of a centered, socially defined, time-bound self, and also beyond the recognized resources of language and confines of literary form' (p.ix). A desire for 'something else', something other than the real, has annihilating effects upon realistic fictional structures. Bersani fully explores the shattering consequences of desire upon literary re-presentation (mostly nineteenth-century) of 'character' as a signifier of social unity. To understand how this fragmentation breaks cultural structures, it is helpful to return to the image of the mirror and to consider its metaphorical use in psychoanalytic theories of the social formation of 'self'.

Bersani stresses the centrality of the mirror as a frequent motif in literature, as a metaphor for the production of other selves. A mirror produces distance. It establishes a different space, where our notions of self undergo radical change. It is 'a spatial representation of an intuition that our being can never be enclosed within any present formulation – any formulation here and now – of our being' (p.208). By presenting images of the self in another space (both familiar and unfamiliar), the mirror provides versions of self transformed into another, become something or someone else. It employs distance and difference to suggest the instability of the 'real' on this side of the looking-glass and it offers unpredictable (apparently impossible) metamorphoses of self into other.

This can be related to Freud's theories of the tripartite development of a 'self' (cf. p.71). First, there is a stage of narcissism (self-love, auto-eroticism), second an attachment to loved objects, and third, a surrender to the laws of necessity, or reality. These stages constitute a process of maturation, producing an 'ego', a 'self', an 'I'. The genesis of the ego is a complex idea and has provoked a lot of theoretical controversy to do with the constitution of the subject through his/her insertion into culture, and his/her simultaneous formation and deformation. It is crucial in considering the complex interaction between ideology and the unconscious life of the individual. Fantasies provide graphic images of this problematic area. The theories of Freud and of Jacques Lacan are indispensable for understanding some of these problems (though it is not always possible to apply their ideas to literary criticism in as neat a manner as this might suggest).[26] The term 'subject' is employed here in preference to 'individual' or 'man' or 'character' to remind us of our subjective positioning within language and within the family: 'self' and 'identity' are not static units or unities.

Lacan's extension of Freudian theory concentrates upon that stage of human development which he terms *le stade du miroir*, the mirror stage. This, in Freud's model, is positioned in the transitional Oedipal stage between primary narcissism (love for self) and attachment to loved objects (love for other), i.e. between his first and second stages of development. Freud sees the child as existing, initially, in a state of undifferentiation, experiencing natural self-love, unseparated and not yet distinguishing between self and other. This distinction 'appears' when a libidinal drive is directed from self to an object external to it: when ego-libido shifts into object-libido. What is formed in this shift is a recognition of self as *object*, as if seen in a mirror, the mirror constituted by the looks of others. This self is the *ego*, and becomes the means of self-definition and identification. The mirror phase effects a shift from the 'body in fragments' and an 'asubjectivity of total presence' (Lacan) to the ideal of a whole body with a unified (constructed) subjectivity. Sexual differentiation follows later, with the establishment of male and female 'identity' during the Oedipal phase, with different entries into the symbolic 'Law of the Father' for the boy and girl child (see Juliet Mitchell's *Psychoanalysis and Feminism*.

Crucial to this theory is its understanding of the ego as a *cultural construction*. Lacan's theory of the ego is analogous to Freud's super-ego, with the *Je-ideal* being the ideal self, or 'I', to which the subject tries to conform, and with which (s)he tries to coincide, since it constitutes his or her identity. Lacan claims that the creation of the ego as an object, as *Je-ideal*, does not sublimate instincts (i.e. divert them into non-sexual, socially valued aims) but represses (i.e. denies) them. Like the super-ego, the 'I' watches, judges, measures and condemns the self as it tries to meet the demands of its social other.

Many fantasies of dualism are dramatizations of precisely this conflict, their 'selves' torn between an original, primary narcissism and an ideal ego, which frustrates their natural desire. Many of them fantasize a return to a state of undifferentiation, to a condition *preceding* the mirror stage and its creation of dualism. For prior to this construction, in a state of primary narcissism, the child is its own ideal, and experiences no discrepancy between self (as perceiving subject) and other (as perceived object). To get back, on to the far side of the mirror, becomes a powerful metaphor for returning to an original unity, a 'paradise' lost by the 'fall' into division with the construction of a subject.

Movement from undifferentiation towards ego-formation effects the subject's insertion in a 'symbolic' order as opposed to an 'imaginary' realm. Julia Kristeva's exposition of Lacan's theories enables us to see this insertion as inseparable from the subject's acquisition of language and 'syntax', by which the social code is created and sustained.

The symbolic is that social order constructed by discrete units of meaning, by a network of signifiers, and it is opposed to the imaginary, which is without (before) signifiers.[27] To break the symbolic by dissolution or deformation of its language (or 'syntax') is taken by Kristeva to be a radical, subversive activity.[28]

The fragmentation of 'character' in fantasy deforms a 'realistic' language of unified, rational selves. The subject becomes ex-centric, heterogeneous, spreading into every contradiction and (im)possibility. 'Fantastic narrative constitutes a decentred discourse of the subject' (Bessière, p.103). Fantastic texts which try to negate or dissolve dominant signifying practices, especially 'character' representation, become, from this perspective, radically disturbing. Their partial and dismembered selves break a 'realistic' signifying practice which represents the ego as an indivisible unit. Fantasies try to *reverse* or rupture the process of ego formation which took place during the mirror stage, i.e. they attempt to re-enter the imaginary. Dualism and dismemberment are symptoms of this desire for the imaginary. 'Corporal disintegration is the reverse of the constitution of the body during the mirror phase, and it occurs only at those times when the unified and transcendent ego is threatened with dissolution' (White, p.10). A fantasy of physical fragmentation corresponds, then, to a breakdown of rational unity. That linguistic order which creates and constitutes a whole self, a total body, is un-done. A non-repressed subject produces unexpected forms of subjectivity, from Frankenstein's monster, to Kafka's man as beetle, or Hélène Cixous's animal productions in *Neutre*: in all of these texts a normalizing identification process is overthrown.

To give representation to an imaginary realm is, however, not possible. This realm is non-thetic, it has no 'human' discourse. To attempt to give it a voice in literature is a manifest contradiction. Nor can human subjects return to that realm without losing their 'humanity', their language. Figures who attempt this return to undifferentiation, in fantastic tales, are doomed to failure. Most versions of the double, for example, terminate with the madness, suicide, or death of the divided subject: 'self' cannot be united with 'other' without ceasing to be. Hence, perhaps, their violence, anger, frustration, energy, dynamic stasis. 'The very means of avoiding reduction to the reflection of things constitutes a desire for the impossible,' writes Bataille, 'unsatisfaction turns into a permanent object' (pp.30, 33).

Literary fantasies from Sade onwards are driven by precisely this kind of restless dissatisfaction. They express a desire for the imaginary, for that which has not yet been caught and confined by a symbolic order, yet the self-mutilation, cruelty, horror and violence which they have to employ to re-turn to the imaginary suggests its inaccessibility. Their awareness of the problem of representing the 'real' draws attention to the relation of signifying practices to that order and its constitution, for with the removal of a fixed notion of 'character', the problem of fictional representation is stressed. A fantastic text tells of an indomitable desire, a longing for that which does not yet exist, or which has not been allowed to exist, the unheard of, the unseen, the imaginary, as opposed to what already exists and is permitted as 'really' visible. Unlike the symbolic, the imaginary is inhabited by an infinite number of selves preceding socialization, before the ego is produced within a social frame. These selves allow an infinite, unnameable potential to emerge, one which a fixed sense of character excludes in advance. Each fantastic text functions differently, depending upon its particular historical placing, and its different ideological, political and economic determinants, but the most subversive fantasies are those which attempt to *transform* the relations of the imaginary and the symbolic. They try to set up possibilities for radical cultural transformation by making fluid the relations between these realms, suggesting, or projecting, the dissolution of the symbolic through violent reversal or rejection of the process of the subject's formation.

# PART TWO:
# TEXTS

# 4 GOTHIC TALES AND NOVELS

I say I am a man, but who is the other who hides in me?
Arthur Machen, *The Great God Pan*

I have said that I dwelt apart from the visible world, but I
have not said that I dwelt alone. This no human creature
may do; for lacking the fellowship of the living, he inevitably draws upon the companionship of things that are
not, or are no longer living.
H.P. Lovecraft, *The Tomb*

As a perennial literary mode, fantasy can be traced
back to ancient myths, legends, folklore, carnival art.
But its more immediate roots lie in that literature of
unreason and terror which has been designated 'Gothic'. It
was with the publication of Horace Walpole's dream novel,
*The Castle of Otranto* (1764), that the demonic found a literary
form in the midst of Augustan ideals of classical harmony,
public decorum and reasonable restraint. Unreason, silenced
throughout the Enlightenment period, erupts in the fantastic art of Sade, Goya and horror fiction. What the classical
period had confined 'was not only an abstract unreason but
also an enormous reservoir of the fantastic. . . . One might
say that the fortresses of confinement added to their social

role of segregation and purification a quite opposite cultural function . . . they functioned as a great, long, silent memory' (Foucault, *Madness and Civilization*, p.210).

Confined to the margins of Enlightenment culture, these 'fortresses of unreason' were both created *by* the dominant classical order and constituted a hidden pressure *against* it. They retained 'an iconographic power that men might have thought was exorcised . . . forbidden figures that could thus be transmitted intact from the sixteenth to the nineteenth century' (ibid.). A massive shift in ideas of order and unreason during the eighteenth century effected a radical transformation of man's perception of himself and of his theories of knowledge.[1] It is in this period that inherited patterns of meaning are lost, with the result that notions of 'reality', of 'human nature', of 'wholeness', are dissolved. There is no link to an absolute meaning, no 'ends', only means without ends.[2] Signs are without transcendent meanings. This period sees the emergence of that disturbingly empty 'fullness' which characterizes modern literature, with its semantic 'emptiness'.

Early Gothic fiction did not explicitly explore these fracturings of meaning, but it did establish a rhetoric of fantasy to be developed by later writers to tell of a loss of signification. Horace Walpole, Clara Reeve, Peter Teuthold, Maria Roche, Anna Barbauld and a plethora of imitators produced hundreds of Gothic novels from 1764 until well into the 1800s, at their most concentrated during the 1780s and 90s. There are several histories and general surveys of Gothic fiction available.[3] David Punter's *The Literature of Terror* (1980) has extended these studies into a comprehensive work on Gothic from Walpole to the present. Gothic is seen as being a reaction to historical events, particularly to the spread of industrialism and urbanization. It is a complex form situated on the edges of bourgeois culture, functioning in a dialogical relation to that culture. But it also conducts a dialogue *within itself*, as it acts out and defeats subversive desires. Hence the difficulty of reading Gothic as politically subversive. 'Gothic fiction demonstrates the *potential* of revolution by daring to speak the socially unspeakable; but the very act of speaking it is an ambiguous gesture' (Punter, p.417). It suggests that the novel, as a genre, requires a certain degree of transgression to sustain it.

There are many different stages in the development of a Gothic tradition, from 'Enlightenment' Gothic to a more internalized psychological narrative. Changes in Gothic can be seen as corresponding to a slow diminution of faith in supernaturalism. Early Gothic romances, such as those of Clara Reeve, are closer to the marvellous than to pure fantasy. Their introduction of supernatural agents – ghosts, magic, animation – to aid human affairs by restoring justice and moral order, reveals a longing for an idealised social order to replace the one which was in the process of being destroyed by emergent capitalism. As Gothic undergoes transformations through the work of Ann Radcliffe, M.G. Lewis, Mary Shelley and Charles Maturin, it develops into a literary form capable of more radical interrogation of social contradictions, no longer simply making up for a society's lacks. It is progressively turned inwards to concern itself with psychological problems, used to dramatize uncertainty and conflicts of the individual subject in relation to a difficult social situation. The subject is no longer confident about appropriating or perceiving a material world. Gothic narrates this epistemological confusion: it expresses and examines personal disorder, opposing fiction's classical unities (of time, space, unified character) with an apprehension of partiality and relativity of meaning.

One of the earliest fantasies of dualism, influencing later Gothic fiction and subsequent tales of people 'in pieces', was Godwin's *Caleb Williams* (1794).[4] It is a disturbingly confused narrative by Caleb, filtering experience through his persecuted vision. On both structural and thematic grounds, it breaks up a unified notion of 'the real'. Caleb, the 'I', the first person narrator, is drawn towards his employer, Falkland, the 'he', object of narration. Falkland is the ideal to which Caleb aspires: 'I have reverenced him ... he was endowed with qualities that partook of divine.' Caleb discovers that this ideal hides criminal instincts: Falkland is revealed as a murderer, and Caleb obsessively pursues his hidden guilt. Guilt cannot be located on either side, for the two 'persons' are one. 'Innocence and guilt are confounded ... he appears to be the persecutor and I the persecuted: is not this difference the mere creature of the imagination?' Since Caleb and Falkland merge together, neither survives as a whole 'character'. Each reflects the other, as one another's 'shadow' and 'plague'. Their fluid identities point to their symbiotic link. Caleb recognizes Falkland's crime to be his own: 'I have been *his* murderer.'

Falkland, the 'he', is Caleb's ideal 'I'. From the moment when Caleb becomes attached to this ideal, there is no possibility of returning to an unknowing self. His link with his reflection gives rise to a complex knot of repression and guilt which he then spends the rest of his life attempting (unsuccessfully) to un-do. Interestingly, Falkland becomes the focal point of a network of hostile forces – that social order which comes into being with the construction of an 'ideal' other. 'My resentment', confesses Caleb, 'was not restricted to my prosecutor, but extended itself to the whole machine of society ... I regarded the whole human species as so many hangmen and torturers ... I cursed the whole system of human existence.' He is unable to reconcile himself to the demands of a repressive social order. He questions the construction of an ideal 'he' – its cost is discovered to be concealing libidinal drives – but he also learns that the consequence of radical questioning (revealing that which should remain hidden) is exclusion from and (real) persecution by social systems. Godwin intended *Caleb Williams* to be a fictional counterpart to his attack upon legal institutions in *Political Justice*. Both are profound questionings of the value of the symbolic (cf. p.90) – one conceptually, one through motifs and forms belonging to a fantasy mode.

Godwin's daughter, Mary Wollstonecraft Shelley, re-works similar problems in her attempts to negate the symbolic. Besides numerous tales dealing with recognizable fantastic devices and themes (of immortality, invisibility, fragmentation, transformation), Mary Shelley wrote two major fantasies, *Frankenstein* (1818) and *The Last Man* (1826). Both of these texts image a desire for something 'other' than the real, without reaching to transcendent solutions. Godwin, especially through his political writings, locates evil in oppressive social institutions – notably the law, and its manipulation by the ruling class. His work shares much of the utopianism of revolutionary texts of the 1790s, retaining an optimism that social conditions could be perfected, but Mary Shelley's writings have lost this faith. They intensify the pessimism of *Caleb Williams*, by presenting the impossibility of resolving internal conflicts generated by cultural institutions. Both *Frankenstein* and *The Last Man* are fantasies of absolute negation or dissolution of cultural order.[5]

The relationship of Frankenstein to his monster reproduces the locked encounter of Caleb and Falkland from Godwin's novel. The monster has no name. It is anonymous, given identity only as Frankenstein's other, his grotesque reflection (hence the common confusion of the monster *as* Frankenstein). It functions as his parodic mirror image. 'My form', mocks the monster, 'is a filthy type of yours, made horrid even from the very resemblance.' Frankenstein tries to read the monster as a supernatural devil, 'I was cursed by some devil, and carried about with me my eternal hell', but it is made by him, self-generated, 'the being whom I had cast among mankind ... my own vampire, my own spirit let loose from the grave and forced to destroy all that was dear to me.' Literally constructed from disintegrated selves – an odd anatomical re-make from corpses as the scientist 'pursues nature to her hiding places' – the monster confronts Frankenstein as his own body in pieces, re-presenting his existence preceding 'the mirror stage', before he acquired a cultural identity. The monster kills Frankenstein's closest friend, 'the image of his former self', as well as his brother, and his sister/bride Elizabeth, on their wedding night, thus 'realizing' a desire for transgression. The interpolated narrative of the monster, unlikely though it seems (with its education into Plutarch, Milton and Goethe), repeats (like a mirror image) Frankenstein's acquisition of language and learning. The monster narrates this acquisition as a terribly painful process –(with its understanding of human language, it learns pain, guilt, and *difference* from others)

*Frankenstein* is much more subtle, though, than an allegory of a man's 'evil' side let loose. What drives the narrative (and what drives *Caleb Williams*) is a strong desire to be unified with this 'other' side. The monster *is* Frankenstein's lost selves, pieces of himself from which he has been severed, and with which he seeks re-unification. Hence his reluctance to kill it. Their relationship is one of love-hatred, and it becomes increasingly exclusive. They have no existence apart from one another. 'The form of the monster on whom I had bestowed existence was for ever before my eyes, and I raved incessantly concerning him.' They are never reconciled. They end in the Antarctic, in a sterile polar region – the condition of their intimacy is a progressive alienation from society – and if they achieve union, it is only through their undifferentiation at death. They can never become one, separation remaining the condition of having a 'human' identity. The open structure of the text, though, protests against this condition. Its ending is really a suspending, as the monster wanders towards the horizon line, its unknown vanishing point, haunting the reader with a sense of uncertainty. It leaves the text unresolved on both thematic and formal levels. 'The fate of all fascination with the self as the other – the fate of a radical open-endedness of being – is a kind of restless immortality' (Bersani, p.212). Dualism is not resolved at the end but is re-located in a final darkness.

According to Robert D. Hume's distinctions between Gothic and Romantic, *Frankenstein* is closer to the first than to the second. In his article 'Gothic versus Romantic', he registers crucial differences between the two forms. Both seek a realization of ideals, but the vision informing Gothic fiction is one lacking faith in organic notions of wholeness, defeating any optimistic faith in progress. Gothic inverts romance structures: the quest, for example, is twisted into a circular journey to nowhere, ending in the same darkness with which it opened, remaining unenlightened. *Frankenstein* marks the establishment of a tradition of disenchanted, secular fantasies, becoming increasingly grotesque and horrific. It is haunted by a loss of absolute meaning, repeating a desire for knowledge and for ultimate truth, but it deflates and deforms this desire through the travestying form of the monster itself, a grotesque parody of the human longing for the more than human. As Hume writes, 'For those who cannot believe in the possible achievement of the ends, the pains of existential discontent loom large . . . Almost schematically, Mary Shelley's novel reverses and denies the Romantic quest for gnosis.' A vast gap is opened up between knowledge (as scientific investigation and rational inquiry) and gnosis (a knowledge of ultimate truths, a kind of spiritual wisdom), and it is in this gap that the modern fantastic is situated.

It is, surely, no accident that *Frankenstein* has become one of the central myths of post-Romantic culture, both through literary and film texts.[6] It lies behind modern fantasy, as an influence and inspiration, but also as an index of the *loss* registered through the fantastic. Frankenstein, as a subject, is driven by a desire for unity with another, by a desire for his life to have absolute significance. Rather than present this desire in transcendental terms, the text of *Frankenstein* remains fully human, fully material. The 'other' who is created by the self is no supernatural or superhuman being, but an amalgam of bodily shreds and patches, a collection of mortal remains, the *disjecta membra* of a dead society raised up again as the living dead. Self as other is recorded here as a grotesque, unredemptive metamorphosis, as mere travesty, parody, horror. It is this reluctance to shift the emphasis from human into superhuman terms which points to *Frankenstein* as a key text behind the modern fantastic. It anticipates Sartre's understanding of such fantasy as being fully human, fully *material*, in its focus upon *matter* and the infiltration of alien matter, its invasion of mind and of body. There is, in such fantasy, what Sartre terms 'a ghost of transcendence floating around in a veil of immanence'. A transition between mind and matter is seen to be possible, but is one in which the mind has no ultimate control, with the result that the self feels itself disassociated and at sea. Thus Gautier's protagonist: 'I dissolved into the object I gazed at, and I myself became that object'.[7] All that the modern fantastic suggests, from *Frankenstein* onwards, is the *impotence* of mind to transcend matter – and the grotesque victory of the latter (found similarly in films of a fantastic genre, such as Romero's *Night of the Living Dead*, Siegel's *Invasion of the Body Snatchers*, Polanski's *Repulsion*, etc.). As Sartre writes:

> The fantastic is an entire world in which things manifest a captive, tormented thought . . . In this world, matter is never entirely matter, since it offers only a completely frustrated attempt at determinism, and mind is never completely mind, because it has fallen into slavery and has been impregnated and dulled by matter . . . *Things suffer and tend towards inertia, without ever attaining it; the debased, enslaved mind unsuccessfully strives towards consciousness and freedom.* ('*Aminadab*', pp.57–8, my italics)

Mary Shelley's other prolonged fantasy, *The Last Man*, is even more extreme as a text unable to imagine a resolution of social contradictions except through complete holocaust. Whereas *Frankenstein* depends upon *Political Justice*, *Caleb Williams*, various utopian fantasies, and Coleridge's *Ancient*

*Mariner*, *The Last Man* depends upon a revolutionary political text, Volney's *Ruins of Empires*. This was an anti-despotic publication, brought over from France to be circulated amongst London's Jacobin circles during the 1790s. It celebrates the destruction of patriarchal empire through death's levelling, and many of its powerful, graphic images provide Mary Shelley with dramatic material: 'And now a mournful skeleton is all that subsists of this opulent city, and nothing remains of its powerful government but a vain and obscure remembrance.' [8]

From this revolutionary material, Mary Shelley constructs a remarkable fantasy of cultural annihilation. It is a long, slow-moving narrative, as it tells of a global plague which spreads gradually across the world. Its panorama of decay presents a complete erasure of the human species. Only Verney, the last man (like Frankenstein's creation of a parodic 'first' man, another inversion of Adam), remains to tell the tale of order lapsing into undifferentiation and decay: it is a vast fantasy of entropy. 'One by one we should dwindle into nothingness.' All civilized forms collapse with the plague's levelling: society becomes amorphous. 'I felt as if, from the order of the systematic world, I had plunged into chaos, obscure, contrary, unintelligible.' Through the plague, ordinary life is uncovered and metamorphosed into its opposite.[9]

Verney, as the last man, mourns for the death of culture, weeping over 'the ruins of the boundless continents of the east, and the desolation of the western world.' It is important to distinguish between his voice, as narrator, and Mary Shelley's position, as author. His human (male) lamentation is not hers. In 'dialogue' with his voice of distress is a huge silence: the plague itself, Mary Shelley's fantasy of annihilation of the human. Her writings open an alternative 'tradition', of 'female Gothic'.[10] They fantasize a violent attack upon the symbolic order and it is no accident that so many writers of a Gothic tradition are women: Charlotte and Emily Brontë, Elizabeth Gaskell, Christina Rossetti, Isak

Dinesen, Carson McCullers, Sylvia Plath, Angela Carter, all of whom have all employed the fantastic to subvert *patriarchal* society – the symbolic order of modern culture.

A remarkable narrative feature of Mary Shelley's texts is their structural indeterminacy. *The Last Man* is a series of 'fragments', the end being left open. *Frankenstein* is similarly indefinite. Structured like a line of receding mirror images, it moves from the outer tale of Walton, to the inner tale of Frankenstein, to the tale-within-the-tale of the monster's confessions. The reader is progressively seduced from a straightforward epistolary 'realism' into the vortex at the centre where the monster is strangely present (i.e. absent), surrounded by the text's webs of language, 'embedded in the innermost circle . . . like the middle ring of a vast inferno' (Goldberg, p.28). The three circles of narrative are not neatly re-situated within each other by the end, but collapse together, as Walton records the progressive vanishing of the monster, its end unknown. This open structure introduces a space within the initial 'closed' realistic form: through the monster, a 'place' has been given to non-human desires.

Jan Potocki's *Saragossa Manuscript* (1804) functions in a similarly distorting manner, and later English Gothic fiction, influenced by German Romanticism, especially Hoffmann's tales, reveals disturbing breaks of normative structure. C.R. Maturin's *Melmoth the Wanderer* (1820), usually regarded as the culmination of English Gothic, is a dramatic example. Its relentlessly fragmented structure permits the reader little security. One scene spirals and merges into another, each tale breaking off to lead towards another tale, equally truncated, incomplete. For all its 'Chinese box structure,' which provoked hostility from literary critics, there is little symmetry. The boxes are not packed together again, but they recede, indefinitely open. The protagonist, Melmoth, is an amalgam of various Romantic avatars: Satan, Faust, Gothic hero/villain, Wandering Jew, Cain. He undertakes an impossible quest to revoke his demonic pact, through seeking a soul sufficiently desperate to take his future place as one of the damned. But it is not a religious parable. The devil, in fact, is notably absent. It is presented only through Melmoth's imaginings, and our magnification of *him* as superhuman: the demonic is generated from the self.

Definitions of the 'real' are manifestly unreliable in *Melmoth*, varying from person to person, so that figures experience themselves as insubstantial – fragmentation, dualism, hallucination, become the norm: 'I saw myself; and this horrid tracing of yourself . . . this haunting of yourself by your own spectre, while you still live is perhaps a curse almost equal to your crimes visiting you in the punishment of eternity.'-[11] Senses are unreliable, 'I had rather trust my dreams than my senses', 'my senses so often deceive me', 'Is it a dream that I see you now? Is it a dream that I talk with you? Tell me, for my senses are bewildered . . . Alas! in the life that I now lead, dreams have become realities, and realities seem only like dreams.'

*Melmoth* is a peculiarly modern text in making problems of perception and representation its subject. It foregrounds difficulties of knowledge and comprehension. 'We ask with the desponding and restless scepticism of Pilate, "what is truth?" but the oracle that was so eloquent one moment, is dumb the next, or if it answers, it is with that ambiguity that makes us dread we have to consult again – again – and for ever – in vain' (p.85). 'We needed a rational interpreter.' 'I neither felt, nor heard, nor understood.' 'What am I to understand from your terrible words?' 'Your words are riddles to me.' 'I do not understand you.' 'You equivocate again . . . you equivocate . . . Your answers are all interrogations or evasions.' The text is labyrinthine, becoming more and more obscure as it pursues an impossible 'clue', 'followed with incessant industry through all its windings of doubt, mystery and disappointment.' Its legendary Faustian figure embodies, on a thematic level, the central issue which is written into the convoluted form of the text: problems of meaning and of interpretation. Faust – and his 'demonic' encounter – enacts, or formalizes, the same quest for an absolute 'reality' embodied by the work's structural fragmentation, its 'truths' receding indefinitely, even as they are apprehended.

Heavily influenced by English Gothic and by German Romanticism – most notably by Hoffmann's *Elixirs of the Devil* (1816) – James Hogg's *Private Memoirs and Confessions of a Justified Sinner* (1824) makes of truth an absolutely impossible object.[12] The narrative is split between an impersonal editor's account and a first-person confession by Robert Wringhim, the sinner. This division of a 'he' and an 'I' only intensifies confusion. A juxtaposition of apparently objective and subjective accounts does not place authority with either of them: it undermines both. Although ostensibly accounts of the same events, they are mutually contradictory, their obliquities refusing, refracting the versions of truth provided elsewhere. By erasing narrative authority, the two versions foreground the unsatisfactory nature of both documented 'fact' and imaginary 'fiction'. The reader is allowed to settle for neither. Constant structural dislocations prevent reader, editor, 'characters', from arriving at a point of stability from which 'truth' may be confirmed.

Any literary re-presentation of 'truth', 'fact', 'history', is thus made problematical in Hogg's fiction. The *Confessions* are close to Bakhtin's idea of a polyphonic, apparently polysemic text (only here, 'meanings' contradict one another), for they mix different literary forms: biography, diatribe, sermon, legend, prayer, myth, editorial comment, theological disputation, confession. Closure (closing the gap between signifier and signified) becomes impossible. An anonymous contemporary reviewer of 1824 registered his objection to this mess: the text, he argued, denies us that 'unity which is essential to the production of a pleasurable impression on the reader'. His resistance anticipates many literary critics' attacks upon forms which are not 'organic', whole, or unified:

> The 'Justified Sinner' will not allow us to jog on comfortably in either character (of believer or philosopher). This inconsistency is as great an annoyance as if the audience were compelled to change their dresses three or four times during a performance instead of the actors.[13]

The structural ambiguity of Hogg's *Confessions*, as with Maturin's *Melmoth*, derives from equivocation as to the nature of the represented object. What constitutes the 'real'? How is it to be known, or told? As with *Melmoth*, these problems revolve around an ambiguous demonic encounter: the 'devil' becomes the figure, in many texts, through which problematic relations to the phenomenal world are articulated. Here, for example, is the 'devil' of natural or supernatural origin? How are the two to be understood and defined? No one character is *sure* of what he or she sees. George Wringhim, 'being confounded between the shadow and the substance, knew not what he was doing or what he had done.' The commonsensical witness, working-class Bella Calvert, despairs at the contradictions offered her: 'We have nothing on earth but our senses to depend on, if these deceive us, what are we to do?' As Blake wrote, 'In an Equivocal World, up and down are Equivocal.' [14]

Equivocation recurs as a verbal *leitmotif* throughout the *Confessions*. Characters and editor are nostalgic for an orthodox demonology which would explain the shadow as a supernatural emanation, but the 'devil' is too equivocal to allow for such a separation. Robert is aware that the strange form is a protean one, assuming the form of the subject whom it doubles: it is variously Robert, George, Colwan, Gil-Martin. Like Hoffman, Hogg is both excited and troubled by an apprehension that the 'I' is more than one. Immanent metamorphosis deprives him of a viable identity, dead shapes seem to be wandering next to him. His only escape from all his multiple 'demons' is suicide.

Dualism is thematically central to nineteenth-century versions of Gothic. There develops a recognizable literature of the double, dualism being one of the literary 'myths' produced by a desire for 'otherness' in this period. The double signifies a desire to be re-united with a lost centre of personality and it recurs as an obsessive motif throughout Romantic and post-Romantic art. Benjamin Constant's *Adolphe* senses his 'unreality', doubles or shadows recur through Hoffmann's *Doppelgänger*, Kleist's *Penthisilea*, Brockden Brown's *Wieland*, Chamisso's *Peter Schlemihl*, anticipating Dickens, Poe, Dostoevsky, Wilde, Stevenson, James and Conrad, all of whom were drawn towards a 'doubling' motif.

Dialogues of self and other are increasingly acknowledged as being colloquies with the self: any demonic presences are generated from within. Schlegel writes that the dialogue used to be conducted with 'God', but is now internalized, so that an 'intrinsic dualism and duplicity' is our condition of being, so that 'we are constrained to recognize our inmost being as essentially dramatic.' [15] There is constant conflict between 'the unwon unity of the two selves', 'at war together'. Hegel similarly saw modern thought as characterized by a quality of doubleness, 'this awareness of the self as the Divided Nature, wherein is only conflict'.[16]

In English and American Gothic, dualism and multiplicity of selves are recurrent 'myths'. American Gothic manifests a similarly slow transition from supernatural to psychological versions of demonic encounter, moving from Brockden Brown, Washington Irving, to Poe, Hawthorne, Melville, James and Faulkner. Before moving on to discuss some texts of dualism in more detail, it is useful to look at Poe's use of the fantastic, for it is in many ways the closest to Sade's extreme. Poe's 'phantasy-pieces' re-work a Gothic topography of enclosures, wastelands, vaults, dark spaces, to express psychic terrors, and primal desires. Like Sade, Poe defies mortal limits, dissolving death through exerting a human will. Transcendence gives way to transgression in Poe's tales of incest and of death's entrance into life, from

*Berenice*, *Morella* and *Ligeia* to *Hop-Frog* and *The Masque of the Red Death*, whose centre is mere vacuity, a 'mask ... untenanted by any tangible form'. *William Wilson*, *Eiros and Charmion*, *Monas and Una* break monistic conceptions of character with their doubles and spectres, whilst *The Pit and the Pendulum* approaches a zero condition of non-being, 'a sense of sudden motionlessness'. Fear is of a void: 'It was not that I feared to look upon things horrible, but that I grew aghast lest there should be *nothing* to see.' [17]

*The Fall of the House of Usher* (1839) is Poe's most famous fantasy. Its narrative method exemplifies that process of 'making strange' which characterizes the uncanny. The tale is introduced through a reflexive frame: a pool of water. Its narrator approaches, then withdraws from, the desolate House of Usher, as a place of death, with its 'bleak walls, vacant eye-like windows, few rank sedges'. The house is not given directly, but as a reflection, i.e. an inverted form of itself in the water of 'a black and lurid tarn' nearby. 'I gazed down – with a shudder ever more thrilling than before – upon the remodelled and inverted images of the gray sedge, and the ghastly tree-stems, and the vacant and eye-like windows.' The 'mansion of gloom' is strangely familiar to him, as he approaches it from 'its image in the pool', both old and new, arousing a dull memory, 'how familiar was all this (yet) how unfamiliar were the fancies which ordinary images were stirring up.' [18] It disturbs him: 'I shuddered knowing not why.' What he encounters is a place where transgression and taboo are permitted: Madeleine and Usher have an incestuous relationship, Madeleine is buried alive and returns from her grave to bring death to Usher. They do not, however, exist as independent characters. They are generated by the narrator, produced through his trance-like condition as he stares into a dirty mirror image, a 'paraxial' realm, on the edge of reality. The house and its inhabitants are 'real' only to the narrator. He re-presents himself as 'other' through Usher, who enacts his fantasy life.

By contrast with Poe's fantasies, Hawthorne's romances

are excessively conceptual: that is, in them, the fantastic is turned into a conceptual scheme and this is characteristic of the tendency to neutralize fantasy (and desire) in a Puritanical culture. Moralizing structures dismiss desire as too fluid, formless and nameless: they categorize and exorcize it as evil. Hawthorne's Faustian stories, such as *The Birthmark*, *Ethan Brand*, *Rappaccini's Daughter*, have the same excessive conceptualization as *The Scarlet Letter* (1850), *The House of the Seven Gables* (1851) and *The Marble Faun* (1860). They try to narrate metamorphoses from self to other, but are constrained by highly structured allegorical schemes.[19] The result of an inveterate allegorizing tendency in Hawthorne is an insistence upon clearly articulated 'meaning', which produces what Jean Normand has termed 'petrified fantasies' (Normand, p.285).

Echoing this *fear* of desire in Hawthorne and many allegorical fantasists and remarkably similar to Poe's *The Fall of the House of Usher* is a little-known tale by William Morris, *Lindenborg Pool* (1856), first published in his *Oxford and Cambridge Magazine*.[20] Its first person narrator stares into a pool, amidst a lonely, dismal landscape, 'trying to learn the secret' of his reflection, like Narcissus. Whilst preoccupied with this mirrored image, he is suddenly, without any rational explanation, transported back from the nineteenth to the thirteenth century. He is accompanied by a strange counterpart, 'a man riding close to me on a horse; he was fantastically dressed . . . striped all over in vertical stripes of yellow and green, with quaint birds, like exaggerated storks . . . counter-changed on the stripes.' This fantastic other conducts him to a medieval castle, where misrule reigns supreme, and all the cultural orders familiar to the narrator collapse. Walls dissolve as rooms merge together to produce 'an endless perspective of gorgeousness'. Metamorphosis – with women dressed as men and men become beasts – laughter, music, eating, dancing, excess, pleasure, are the norm. Morris's Victorian time-traveller experiences confusion and panic:

[they] began to move about, in a bewildering dance-like motion, mazy and intricate . . . people talking and singing and laughing and twirling about, till my brain went round and round, and I scarce knew what I did; yet somehow, I could not leave off; I dared not even look over my shoulder, fearing lest I should see something so horrible as to make me die. (p.156)

All that he most fears takes form as a dying man who refuses a Christian blessing (like Sade's obdurate atheist in 'A dialogue between a priest and a dying man') and is metamorphosed into a pig – the 'natural' shape of his inhumanity, or immorality:

with a sound that was half snarl, half grunt . . . a huge *swine* that I had been shriving tore from me the Holy Thing, deeply scoring my hand as he did so with tusk and tooth, so that the red blood ran quick on to the floor. (p.156)

The castle is perceived as 'a ghastly place', threatening with non-existence 'that which I counted so holy'. It offends human order and the narrator's faith. 'All sacredest things even were made a mock of.' 'These things are strangely like devils.' Fearing to lose what he calls 'self', the narrator flees back to his Victorian life of 'duty', prayer, penance, stillness. He hallucinates the collapse of his fantasy world:

Then I arose and turned to go, but even as I did so I heard a roar as if the world were coming in two, and looking toward the castle, saw, not a castle, but a great cloud of white lime-dust swaying this way and that in the gusts of the wind. (p.157)

in a manner which is remarkably close to the fall of the mansion in Poe's tale: 'my brain reeled as I saw the mighty walls rushing asunder . . . and the deep and dark tarn at my feet closed sullenly and silently over the fragments of the "HOUSE OF USHER" ' (p.157). Both Poe and Morris construct and then collapse a 'paraxial' realm, where transgression is the norm. Their narrators enter and return from it: Morris's with a fear of its non-thetic fluidity, its pleasures of undifferentiation, music, laughter, sensuality. He can contain their threat only by reading them as diabolical and re-writing them as forbidden, taboo subjects. He is left still 'trying to fathom the Lindenborg Pool'.

/As Victorian horror fiction evolves, it reveals a gradual apprehension of the demonic as mere absence, rather than as essentially diabolic. Between *Frankenstein* and *Jekyll and Hyde* there occurred a shift, which gave a different 'name' to unfamiliar aspects of the self. One index of this transition is found in the fantasies of Bulwer Lytton, from his Byronic tale *Falkland* (1827) and *Zanoni* (1842) to *A Strange Story* (1862). Despite their tediously long passages of occult philosophy, Lytton's tales begin to recognize a disturbing feature of modern Gothic: that the object of fear can have no adequate representation and is, therefore, all the more threatening. 'It' is something without a name, without a form. Because it is unnameable, it is not easily exorcized. It exists prior to nomination as good or evil. Lytton's Dr Fenwick refers to 'it' as negating *the something* without which men could never found cities, frame laws, bind together, beautify, exalt the elements of this world.' [21] Pure negativity, 'It was a Darkness shaping itself out of the air in very undefined outline . . . its dimensions seemed gigantic.[22] Lytton's works hunt down 'the presence of the Nameless', the 'shapeless, formless, nameless', 'unutterable Horror', 'that Dark Thing, whatever it might be', which they summon, renouncing the very space they uncover as being a threat to social order. But Lytton's fiction remains rather abstract: it is left to Wilde and Stevenson to use this apprehension of an a-moral, non-signifying horror in more immediate fantasies.

Oscar Wilde's *The Picture of Dorian Gray* (1891) is closer to a faery than a fantastic mode, for it is structured around a 'wish-come-true' device. Dorian's desire to remain beautiful, whilst his painted portrait suffers his proper ravaging by time, is fulfilled. His picture is an ideal reproduction of himself, self as perfect other, and he assumes the appearance of this ideal. But their roles are confused. With their exchange (Wilde's secular version of a demonic pact), the portrait functions as the ideal ego, reminding Dorian of his guilt, his responsibilities, his immorality, whilst he only seeks immortality for his beauty. The picture, his ideal, is all that he has fallen from.

> But the picture? What was he to say to that? It held the secret of his life, and told his story. It had taught him to love his own beauty. Would it teach him to loathe his own soul? . . . It was watching him, with its beautiful marred face and its cruel smile . . . The picture, changed or unchanged, would be to him the visible emblem of conscience . . .[23]

Dorian comes to detest being trapped by his narcissism. He has 'a grotesque dread of mirrors and polished metal surfaces and still water' and tries to smash the mirror which traps him (as image) behind it: 'flinging the mirror on the floor [he] . . . crushed it into silver splinters beneath his heel'.

Dorian's dualism begins as defiant self-realization. He takes up the challenge of Lord Henry Wotton, who declares that 'even the bravest man amongst us is afraid of himself. The mutilation of the savage has its tragic survival in the self-denial that mars our lives . . . your soul grows sick with longing for the things it has forbidden to itself, with desire for what its monstrous laws have made monstrous and unlawful' (p.26). Dorian transgresses these laws by fulfilling all his sexual desires and even by murder, yet far from escaping social pressures, he is trapped more tragically by their subtle mediation to him through his reflection, his portrait. He cannot escape this emblem of conscience, for it is himself. 'I am too much concentrated on myself. My own personality has become a burden to me. I want to escape, to go away, to forget.' He cannot release himself.

> The double turns out to be a functional expression of the psychological fact that an individual with an attitude of this kind cannot free himself from a certain phase of his narcissistically loved ego development. He encounters it always and everywhere. (Rank, *The Double: A Psychoanalytic Study*, p.80)

Dorian's 'self' can be left only by ceasing to be: self as other is destroyed when he stabs the painted canvas, thus fatally wounding himself. A 'passion for impossible things', even through Wilde's fantasy, is doomed to failure: Dorian cannot retain his primary narcissism. Unable to go through the mirror (stage), Dorian is left to fall back from the burden of self by ceasing to have any human life.

Another famous parable of dualism, R.L. Stevenson's *The Strange Case of Dr Jekyll and Mr Hyde* (1896), is usually seen as the clearest allegory of Victorian hypocrisy and repression: 'Behind its latterday Gothick lies a very profound and epoch-revealing truth.' [24] The other side of the human returns to act out latent libidinal drives concealed by the social ego. (Je-kyll – I kill – his very name has within it his real nature as murderer, embodied in Hyde – what is hidden.) This exemplifies Freud's theory of fantastic narrative as telling of a return of the repressed: Hyde is able to fulfil Jekyll's desires to steal, love, be violent. As with Lytton's fantasies, though, Stevenson's is much more than an allegory of good and evil at war with one another. The text itself draws attention to 'evil' as a relative moral category, as a notion imposed upon natural disorder. Jekyll, conducting his 'experiment while under the empire', is drawn towards the world on the other side of the mirror because it offers him an infinite number of 'selves'. He regards a monistic definition of character as limited: man is not only dipsychic, but polypsychic, endlessly 'other':

> man is not truly one, but truly two. I say two, because the state of my own knowledge does not pass beyond that point (but) I hazard the guess that man will be ultimately

known for a mere polity of multifarious, incongruous and independent denizens.[25]

Good-evil dichotomies are preceded by an a-moral condition, one which echoes Sade's ideal of undifferentiation, his 'universal prostitution of all beings'. Jekyll is attracted to this ideal as his original, undivided nature.

Hence it came about that I concealed my pleasures . . . I already stood committed to a profound duplicity of life . . . When I looked upon that ugly idol in the glass, I was conscious of no repugnance, rather of a leap of welcome. This, too, was myself. It seemed natural and human. In my eyes it bore a livelier image of the spirit, it seemed more express and single, than the imperfect and divided countenance I had been hitherto accustomed to call mine. (pp. 48, 51)

Hyde is originally a nameless, shapeless thing, without identity, smaller than Jekyll, dwarflike, *within* his parent's form. He is 'hardly human! Something troglodytic, shall we say? . . . Like a man restored from death . . . he gave an impression of deformity without any nameable malformation' (p.13). The lawyer, Utterson, reads into Hyde's face 'Satan's signature' and Jekyll refers to him as 'that child of hell', though initially Hyde was 'neither diabolical nor divine', but prior to human concepts of good and evil. Hyde introduces absolute otherness, 'a sense of unreality', an a-morality beneath moral structures. 'As for the moral turpitude that man *unveiled* to me . . . I cannot dwell on it without a sense of horror.' Hyde threatens late Victorian London with his horrid laughter, theft, sexuality, criminality: he breaks every social taboo. What most frightens Jekyll is Hyde's distance from the human, his non-human origins, i.e. his link with the inorganic, which comes to be categorized as demonic in an 'evil' sense:

he thought of Hyde, for all his energy of life, as of something not only hellish but inorganic. This was the

shocking thing; that the slime of the pit seemed to utter
cries and voices; that the amorphous dust gesticulated
and sinned; that what was dead, and had no shape,
should usurp the office of life. And this again, that that
insurgent horror was knit to him closer than a wife, closer
than an eye . . . (it) prevailed against him, and deposed
him out of life. (p.61)

Once this inorganicism is recognized, the text has to evolve
strategies to contain and exclude it. *Dr Jekyll and Mr Hyde*
develops in the pattern of the detective novel 'hunting
down' anti-social energies, neutralizing desire. The relation
of Jekyll to Hyde is also one of father to son. 'Jekyll had
more than a father's interest; Hyde had more than a son's
indifference.' Like other fantasies, this one repeats the Oedipal drama of father-son conflict and finally rewrites the
victory of the first.

Fantasies of recidivism (a relapse into crime) multiplied in
Victorian England after the publication of Darwin's *Origin
of Species* (1859). A pull towards a state of entropy seemed to
have been given biological justification: this was the state
from which the human had slowly emerged and to which it
was inclined to return. Recidivism and regression to bestial
levels are common post-Darwinian fantasies. Arthur
Machen's *The Great God Pan* (1894) tells of evolution
reversed, human beings slowly sinking backwards towards
animality, becoming the 'other' they always had been.

Reduction to a primal state of inorganicism, of the pre-
human, is equally horrific to Machen and to H.G. Wells,
whose fantasies shrink from all that is not human. Wells's
two best fantasies, *The Island of Doctor Moreau* (1896) and *The
Invisible Man* (1897), are situated between his naturalistic
novels, like *Kipps* or *The History of Mr Polly*, and science
fictions, such as *The Time Machine, The War of the Worlds, Men
like Gods, The Sleeper Wakes*. Through a fantasy mode, Wells
un-covers an *absence* of value which is re-covered in his
mimetic and marvellous fictions, with their social and

cosmic images of order. *Dr Moreau* and *The Invisible Man*, by contrast, are more clearly aligned to a tradition of Gothic horror, one which questions the viability of a bourgeois ideology and invalidates assertions of universal goodness or justice.

*The Island of Dr Moreau* reproduces *Frankenstein* and echoes *Jekyll and Hyde*: its titulary 'mad' scientist seeks to create human life, but his quest becomes its own parody. Moreau's idealism is deflated by the travesties he produces. He transplants features from different beasts, trying to pull them to a human shape, but his speeding up of Darwin's evolutionary process fails. 'I fell short,' he confesses, 'of the things I dream (. . .) There is a kind of travesty of humanity over there.' [26] A lapse of the human back to the pre-human is brilliantly realized through a dream-like sequence, as everything reverses to 'a kind of generalized animalism.' 'Day by day', records Prendick as he watches Moreau's creatures lapse to bestiality, 'the human semblance left them.' It is the loss of decent, bourgeois codes of behaviour which really offends him. There is a loss of human articulacy: syntax dissolves. 'Can you imagine language, once clear-cut and exact, softening and guttering, losing shape and import, becoming mere lumps of sound again?' The monsters lose their upright position, sinking from vertical to horizontal postures. What is worse, the females 'disregard the injunction of decency', for they 'even attempted public outrages upon the institution of monogamy.' Prendick is unable to 'pursue this disagreeable subject'. 'The tradition of the law was clearly losing its force', he records, with people becoming 'commoner every day'.

What Prendick discovers upon the island is his own sense of nihilism. He reads there his own 'loss of faith in the sanity of the world' and finds nothing but 'A blind fate, a vast pitiless mechanism (which) seemed to cut and shape the fabric of existence.' His return to London only disguises this 'terror', the 'shadow' over his soul. He experiences difficulty approaching 'his fellow creatures' who seem mere 'dead bodies', he has 'no desire to return to mankind'. He had been drawn to the 'uncanny voices' of the island as non-human utterances, but as Wells's humanism triumphs, he is recalled. He retains, though, an obdurate sense of an imaginary other world, however horrific, which haunts him as a reminder of all that humanism has excluded.

Bram Stoker's *Dracula* (1897) follows these horrific tales of Stevenson and Wells to provide a culmination of nineteenth-century English Gothic. It engages with a similar desire for and dismissal of transgressive energies. The consequences of a longing for immortality from a merely human context are horrifically realized by Dracula, who is not content with a promise of eternal life elsewhere. He dissolves the life/death boundary, returning from an otherworld to prey upon the living. He occupies a paraxial realm, neither wholly dead nor wholly alive. He is a present absence, an unreal substance. Dr Van Helsing points out that Dracula produces no mirror image. 'He throws no shadow; he makes in the mirror no reflect' (p.203). He is beyond organic life. 'This Thing is not human – not even beast', writes Jonathan Harker. 'I was beginning to shudder at the presence of this being, this Un-dead . . . and to loathe it.' Dracula comes from an inorganic realm, before cultural formation. 'The very place', says Helsing, 'where he have been alive [sic], Undead for all these centuries, is full of strangeness of the geologic and chemical world. There are deep caverns and fissures that reach none know whither.'

Dracula's victims share his un-dead quality. They become parasites, feeding off the real and living, condemned to an eternal interstitial existence, *in between* things: 'We all looked on in horrified amazement as we saw the woman, with a corporeal body as real at that moment as our own, pass in through the interstice where scarce a knife-blade could have gone!'[27] Like the elusive demon of Hogg's *Confessions*, Dracula has no fixed form. He metamorphoses as bat, rat, rodent, man. He is without scruple, without form. His appearance means that chaos is come again, for he is *before*

good or evil, outside human categorization. The text is never completely 'naturalized' as a moral allegory. Van Helsing realizes that Dracula is the inverse side of his legality, that only a thin line separates them. Adapted from Herzog's film version of the tale, Paul Monette's *Nosferatu*[28] emphasizes this symbiotic link, for Harker *becomes* Dracula. The 'other', the vampire, is a reflection of the self. Harker's name suggests it is his *listening* which calls up the vampire as his echo. He admits a vague familiarity with the female vampire who visits him. 'I seemed somehow to know her face, and to know it in connection with some dreamy fear . . . a longing and at the same time some deadly fear.' *Dracula* remains one of the most extreme inversions of Christian myth and subversions of Victorian morality. It blasphemes against Christian sacraments – Renfield, the count's disciple, chants 'The blood is the life! The blood is the life!' It offends sexual taboos. Not only the count, but also his female converts, return like repressed memories to suck away life: the sexual undertones are barely concealed.

*Dracula* – and any vampire myth – is also a re-enactment of that killing of the primal father who has kept all the women to himself – a pattern which is found in ancient mythology, as Freud elaborated in *Totem and Taboo*. Fraternal groups, he wrote, at some stage banded together to murder and devour the father who had retained the right to keep various women to himself. 'The violent primal father had doubtless been the feared and envied model of each one of the company of brothers: and in the act of devouring him they accomplished their identification with him, and each one of them acquired a portion of his strength.' [29] The close link between Van Helsing and Count Dracula in Stoker's version points to this identification – indeed, the fantasizing activities of the whole novel point to a barely concealed *envy* for the count's erotic and sadistic and appropriating pleasures. By defeating these desires, the narrative reasserts a prohibition on exogamy. An excellent article by Richard Astle has explored in greater detail the ways in which

*Dracula* enacts a killing of the father and re-enacts the process of the subject's insertion into human culture, borrowing from Freud and Lacan to deepen the argument.[30]

The vampire myth is perhaps the highest symbolic representation of eroticism. Its return in Victorian England (drawing upon legendary material, Polidori's *Vampyr*, the popular *Varney the Vampire* and implicit vampiric elements of *Frankenstein*) points to it as a myth born out of extreme repression. It is during his period of engagement to Lucy that Harker enters the world of Dracula and vampirism: a bourgeois family structure, to which his engagement is the key, gives rise to its own undead, suggesting that the law contains, through repression, its 'other'. The fantasy of vampirism is generated at the moment of maximum social repression: on the eve of marriage (a similar balance is established in *Frankenstein*, when the monster murders Elizabeth on the wedding night). It introduces all that is 'kept in the dark': the vampires are active *at night*, when light/vision/the power of the *look* are suspended.

What is represented in the vampiric myth in *Dracula* is a symbolic *reversal* of the Oedipal stage and of the subject's cultural formation in that stage. In relation to the theories of Lacan previously introduced it could be claimed that the act of vampirism is the most violent and extreme attempt to negate, or reverse, the subject's insertion into the symbolic. The vampiric act is divided into two: firstly, a penetration of the victim with canine (phallic) teeth; secondly, a sucking of the victim's (life-supporting) blood. The first re-enacts the subject's insertion into the order of the phallus (father), through reversal; the second implies that through such negation, a return has been established to the pre-Oedipal stage, replacing the subject in a symbiotic relation to the mother (the blood sucking repeats sucking at the breast as well as the condition of being provided with life-as-blood inside the womb). With each penetration and 'return' to the unity of the imaginary, a new vampire is produced: further objects of desire are endlessly generated, creating an 'other' order of beings, for whom desire never dies and whose desire prevents them from dying – hence the subversive power of the vampire myth and a consequent recourse to magic and mechanical religious rites (the stake through the heart, the crucifix) to fix and defeat desire. The sadistic piercing of the vampire with the stake re-asserts the rule of the father, re-enacting the original act of symbolic castration visited upon the subject for desiring union with the mother. Stoker's version of the myth repeats this castration, and rids the world at the same time of all non-bourgeois elements.

The ideological implications of having Lucy and Mina as the vulnerable bodies of the text hardly need spelling out. Stoker's sexual and political position is rather more conspicuous in his less successful fantasies, such as *The Lair of the White Worm* (1914).[31] This exorcises evil incarnated in a black servant, Oolanga, and a violent female, Arabella, both being sadistically destroyed. Arabella *is* the white worm, interestingly both snake-like and without colour (i.e. life); threatening an aristocratic and male-dominated world, she/it is necessarily sacrificed for the preservation of patriarchy.

Very clearly with *The Lair of the White Worm*, but equally so with *Dracula*, Stoker reinforces social, class, racial and sexual prejudices. His fantasies betray the same tendency as many Victorian texts: they manipulate apparently non-political issues into forms which would serve the dominant ideology. Like Wells, Stevenson, Lytton and mainstream novelists, Stoker identifies the protean shadow of the 'other' as evil. In the guise of its 'unnameable' absolute otherness, social realities are deformed and dismissed. The shadow on the edges of bourgeois culture is variously identified, as black, mad, primitive, criminal, socially deprived, deviant, crippled, or (when sexually assertive) female. Difficult or unpalatable social realities are distorted through many literary fantasies to emerge as melodramatic shapes: monsters, snakes, bats, vampires, dwarfs, hybrid beasts, devils, reflections, *femmes fatales*. Through this identification, troublesome social elements can be destroyed in the name of exorcising the demonic. Many fantasies play upon a *natural* fear of formlessness, absence, 'death', to reinforce an *apparently 'natural'* order of life – but that order is in effect an arbitrary one which identifies the 'norm' as a middle-class, monogamous and male-dominated culture. In the name of defeating the 'inhuman', such fantasies attempt to dismiss forces inimical to a bourgeois ideology.

Fantasies are never ideologically 'innocent' texts. The tradition of Gothic fiction, traced here from *Frankenstein* to *Dracula*, in many ways reinforces a bourgeois ideology. Many of its best known texts reveal a strong degree of social and class prejudice and it goes without saying, perhaps, that they are heavily misogynistic. Yet the drive of their narratives is towards a 'fantastic' realm, an imaginary area, preceding the 'sexed' identity of the subject and so introducing repressed female energies and absent unities. Especially in the vampire myth, the attempt to *negate* cultural order by *reversing* the Oedipal stage constitutes a violent countercultural thrust which then provokes further establishment of repression to defeat, or castrate, such a thrust. The centre of the fantastic text tries to break with repression, yet is inevitably constrained by its surrounding frame. Such contradictions emerge in graphic form in the many Gothic and fantastic episodes which break into nineteenth-century novels, erupting into the calm surface and bland face of their realism with disturbing reminders of things excluded and expelled. These contradictions will be examined in the next chapter.

# 5 FANTASTIC REALISM

But the civilized human spirit, whether one calls it
bourgeois or merely leaves it at civilized, cannot get rid of
a feeling of the uncanny . . .

> Thomas Mann, *Doctor Faustus*

Perhaps, also, you will come to believe that real life is
more singular and more fantastic than anything else and
that all a writer can really do is present it as 'in a glass,
darkly'.

> E.T.A. Hoffmann, *The Sandman*

IT would be misleading to regard fantasy as an 'alternative' literary form during the nineteenth century. Not
only were writers like Kingsley and Carroll well-
established figures, but mainstream novelists, working
primarily with realistic conventions, also relied upon non-
realistic modes. Gothic, sensationalism, melodrama,
romance, fantasy, disrupt a 'monological' vision, fracturing
the texts of Charlotte and Emily Brontë, Dickens, Balzac,
Wilkie Collins, Dostoevsky, Hardy, James, Conrad, etc.
Flaubert's *Rêve d'enfer* and *La tentation de St Antoine* incline
towards fantasy. Even George Eliot, notably in her story *The
Lifted Veil*, reworks Gothic horror. From a Marxist perspec-

tive, such an intrusion of fantastic sequences constitutes an interrogation of the ideals sustained through bourgeois realism. 'The fissuring of organic form becomes a progressive act': 'In English literary culture of the past century, the ideological basis of organic form is peculiarly visible, as a progressively impoverished bourgeois liberalism attempts to integrate more ambitious and affective ideological modes.' [1]

An uneasy assimilation of Gothic in many Victorian novels suggests that within the main, realistic text, there exists another non-realistic one, camouflaged and concealed, but constantly present. Analogous to Freud's theory of the workings of the Unconscious, this inner text reveals itself at those moments of tension when the work threatens to collapse under the weight of its own repression. These moments of disintegration, of incoherence, are recuperated with difficulty. They remain as an obdurate reminder of all that has been silenced in the name of establishing a normative bourgeois realism. A dialogue between fantastic and realistic narrative modes often operates within individual texts, as the second attempts to repress and defuse the subversive thrust of the first. This dialogue is equivalent, on the level of narrative form, to the dialogue of self and other which is thematically central to nineteenth-century literature. A fear of immanent metamorphosis from 'real' to 'unreal' increases the stranglehold of dominant notions of 'reality' and their fictional reproduction. Ironically, a Gothic tradition is increasingly employed to serve and not to subvert a dominant ideology. Its horrors, transgression and sexual 'licence' are exploited by many Victorian novelists to deter a bourgeois reading public from political revolution, even as it provides them with a temporary fulfilment of ungratified desire.

Formal contradictions are particularly evident in reworkings of Gothic by the Brontës, Elizabeth Gaskell and Charles Dickens. Charlotte Brontë's *Jane Eyre* (1847), *Shirley* (1849), *Villette* (1853), are heavily saturated with Gothic, expressing a violent dissatisfaction with oppressive social forms through Gothic horror, sensationalism, dream, 'surrealism'.[2] *Jane Eyre* and *Villette* continue that tradition which Ellen Moers terms 'female Gothic', providing virulent invectives against patriarchal society. Jane Eyre and Lucy Snowe (both orphans, i.e. fantasies of being without origins) are isolated women seeking emotional and sexual fulfilment, but they are unable to create 'whole' selves within a hostile male order. They remain partial, disintegrated. Part of Jane is externalized as the 'mad' Bertha Mason, whose female passions, anger, energy and resentment are locked away by the romantic (Byronic) figure of Rochester. Bertha remains confined to the attics of Thornfield Hall until she is almost consumed (by her own fire) and has to leap to her death. Jane cannot be reconciled with this demonic, desiring, 'other' side of herself.[3] Her final union with a severely maimed and blinded Rochester suggests that cultural survival is at the cost of extreme curtailment of desire. (Elizabeth Barrett Browning reproduces this plot, with similar implications, in her long poem *Aurora Leigh*.)[4] Lucy Snowe's passions are equally denied. A strange, ghost-like nun, revived from the bleeding nun legend of many Gothic novels, haunts Lucy with a reminder of her own death-in-life (her name indicates whiteness, sterility), but even as she makes claims on life, it recedes from her. To call these novels sado-masochistic fantasies, as some critics have, is to neglect Charlotte Brontë's constrained historical situation. Desires expressed through Gothic sequences in her novels are violently repressed as she returns the reader to a world without illusions or great expectations.

Gothic episodes of fever, nightmare and horror recur similarly at crucial moments of *Shirley*, relating a lacerated female psyche to working-class oppression. Caroline Helstone and Shirley Keeldar make violent protests against women's subordination (Caroline through psychosomatic illness, Shirley through articulate verbal attacks), coinciding with the text's minimal representation of outbreaks of revolutionary violence. Luddite rioters smash the property belonging to the man with whom Shirley and Caroline are involved: property and patriarchy are linked together. Attacks on both are silenced by the novel's romance ending; as Caroline wryly comments, 'I observe that to such grievances as society cannot readily cure, it usually forbids utterance.'[5]

Elizabeth Gaskell's *Mary Barton* (1848) functions similarly. A predominantly realistic narrative suddenly spirals through fantastic interludes of unreason, dream, violence, sexual desire, revolutionary activity, only to sink back towards a quiescent happy ending. Mary's temporary outbreak of desire for self-realization runs parallel to a Chartist uprising, both being contained by a restoration of a 'normal' state of affairs, through marriage and a compromise of class conflict in Evangelical peace.

Elizabeth Gaskell's reputation has traditionally rested upon *Mary Barton* and such classic novels as *Cranford, North and South, Wives and Daughters*, but her image is rather different in her less well-known Gothic pieces. Gaskell seems to be drawn towards the fantastic as a mode which permits her to express disillusionment with ideals of historical progress. An ineradicable morbid streak is dramatically apparent through her ghostly and ghastly tales of estrangement, haunting, isolation, fear, sexual victimization, suicide and murder, most of which were first published by Dickens in his periodical *Household Words* (1850–9). *The Grey Woman, The Doom of the Griffiths, The Half-Brothers, The Crooked Branch, The Sexton's Hero, Lizzie Leigh, Disappearance, Lois the Witch, The Old Nurse's Story, Clopton House, The Well of Pen-Morfa, Curious if True, The Squire's Story* are fantasies revealing a profound dissatisfaction with cultural possibilities. They operate in marked contrast to the optimistic promises of social progress against which they emerged in England of the 1850s and 60s. They do not reappropriate their hostility to ruling assumptions by collapsing all tensions together in the kind of 'happy ending' which terminates Gaskell's more 'realistic' fiction.

*The Grey Woman*, first published by Dickens's *All the Year Round* (January, 1861), presents a young wife who has been deserted. She exists, half-alive, in perpetual torpor. 'There I lived in the same deep retirement, never seeing the light of day . . . my yellow hair was grey, my complexion was ashen-coloured, no creature could have recognized [me]. . . . They called me The Grey Woman.' She has metamorphosed from self to other because, as an abandoned woman, she has no place within society. Without an identity given to her by her position as a wife, she does not signify: she is mere absence. Hence her retreat to an 'other' spectral region. She fears she will 'never entirely recover'. 'Every prop' gives way. She is a 'doomed victim'. Gothic persecution and a shadowy topography is used by Gaskell – as by Charlotte Brontë and Mary Shelley – to tell of a withdrawal from the symbolic order. Her fantasy is a form of protest against patriarchy.[6]

*Six Weeks at Heppenheim*, published by *Cornhill Magazine* (May, 1862) is another of Gaskell's tales of estrangement. Its narrator is inexplicably paralysed: he is suddenly unable to move. 'I was almost surprised myself at my *vis inertiae*. . . . I was disinclined to move, or even to speak . . . the darkness brought out shadows that perplexed me.' As a fantasy of physical immobilization, this tale anticipates Kafka's *Metamorphosis*: the subject's paralysis can only be 'read' as his reluctance to engage with a cultural order which he finds hostile. Withdrawal into a fantasy world does not function here as a compensatory activity, but as protest against a life-denying 'reality'. Through her bleak Gothic sequences, Gaskell emerges as a writer who does not seek to transcend that reality but to erode and re-form it.

*Lois the Witch* is one of Gaskell's purest Gothic tales. Lois is exiled from a familiar English world by the death of her parents. Cut off from her origins, she emigrates to America and her new 'family' accuses her of being a witch. (As a fantasy of persecution, it again anticipates Kafka.) Lois has no means of resisting their attacks. She cannot prove that she is not 'other', for they are determined to 'read' her as a demonic threat. She is expelled, imprisoned, sentenced to death, without rhyme or reason. Neither her life nor her death signifies. She has 'no place', as woman, as stranger, as designated 'evil', and she is sacrificed to confirm a society's prejudices.[7] 'Witch Lois! she is a witch, abhorred of all men . . . men must have hated her bitterly before they could have treated her thus.' Gaskell makes no concessions here to implicit demands for optimistic resolutions. Lois's ending is one of sheer despair: 'Directly afterwards, the body of Lois the Witch swung in the air.' None of Gaskell's 'fantastic' tales is trapped by that ideological frame which determines the endings of her novels. Here, she is able to declare her disbelief that cultural engagement might offer redemption or integration for her isolated (usually female) subjects. Unlike her novels, Gaskell's fantasies terminate in death, or are suspended upon an image of endless withdrawal from the 'real'.

A classic fantasy of existence without familiar human origins is Emily Brontë's *Wuthering Heights* (1847), a text which points to the impossibility of realizing desire within a given culture. Heathcliff, as an outsider whose social roots are unknown, is called variously 'a mad dog', 'an incarnate goblin', 'an unreclaimed creature, without refinement, without cultivation', 'a fierce, pitiless, wolfish man'. Critics who read Lautréamont's *Maldoror* or Stoker's *Dracula*, Stevenson's *Jekyll and Hyde*, or Lewis's *The Monk* as fantasies bringing about a welcome defeat of the 'barbaric' and 'inhuman' need to be aware that Brontë's Heathcliff belongs to the same realm of absolute 'otherness'. To expel *their* demonism is to expel all that Heathcliff signifies in terms of passion, vitality, exuberance, energy.

Heathcliff is all that the other characters are not. He is closer to the demonic than to the human, but he is not supernatural. He is self become other. He and Cathy are two non-identical doubles, reflections of a unified self. Each regards the other as the self transformed. Cathy declares 'I *am* Heathcliff', and their quest is to regain their essential unity. Bersani's study of *Wuthering Heights* examines the various narrative strategies evolved to expel desire from the text. Two narrators, Lockwood and Nelly Dean, try to interpret Heathcliff as devil and madman. Lockwood asks 'Is Mr Heathcliff a man? If so, is he mad? And if not, is he a devil?', whilst Nelly Dean echoes, 'Is he a ghoul, or a vampire? I had read of such hideous, incarnate demons . . . the little dark thing, harboured by a good man to his bane.' [8]

Lockwood (his name signifies closure, tightness, repression) dare not admit Heathcliff and Cathy into his world, i.e. (since he is narrator) into the world of the novel. He shuts out Cathy's homeless ghost, violently rubbing her bare wrist on a jagged edge of glass at the window, until the blood runs. The second half of the text constructs complex genealogical bonds between all the characters to intensify the exclusion of Heathcliff as other. It is a terribly frenetic construction of family ties, distancing the threat of the non-familial, the unfamiliar. 'Narrative structure works towards the expulsion of difference', writes Bersani. 'Structural circularity and repetitiveness . . . finally leaves no room for Heathcliff . . . the domestic is a defence against the alienating metamorphosis' (pp. 202, 211). The family excludes everything foreign to itself as being unnatural. It guarantees ontological stability through limitation and closure. By the end of *Wuthering Heights*, the threat represented by Heathcliff and Cathy has been exorcised by confining it to their own vampiric relationship: they are mere restless spirits drifting around the abandoned enclosure of the Heights.

As Bersani amply demonstrates, problems of social integration, of restraining desire (which threatens to disintegrate social and narrative forms) are worked out through many nineteenth-century texts. Novels tend to enclose desire within structures focussed around the family, itself produced and sustained by taboos against libidinal drives. Fantasy, as a literature of the 'uncanny' in this period, brought to the surface unconscious desire and threatened to dissolve those taboos. Hardly surprisingly, fantasy was pushed to the edges of the novel, where its radical opposition to the 'natural' order (established through a 'realistic' mode of representation) was rendered relatively harmless. Bersani takes as paradigmatic of this narrative pattern one of Balzac's works, *La peau de chagrin* (translated as *The Wild Ass's Skin*). Balzac uses non-realistic modes – fantasy and allegory – to tell of the effects of desire in his tales. *La peau de chagrin*, *La recherche de l'absolu*, *Seraphita* and *Louis Lambert* all tell of cases of Faustian over-reaching. *La Peau de chagrin* is close to a fairy story (like *Dorian Gray*) for it permits its hero, Raphael, to realize all his wishes through a magical skin. 'This is a talisman which fulfils my desires and represents my life-span.' [9] But each satisfaction causes the skin to shrink and Raphael's life to become shorter. Pauline, his lover, causes his death precisely through her desire for him. Raphael's choice represents allegorically a conflict encountered through many nineteenth-century fantasies as they enter and collide with realistic forms: a choice of desire without life, or of life without desire.

This conflict is written into Dickens's novels with their polyphonic mixing of realistic, grotesque, comic, fantastic, and horrific styles. Through their Gothic sequences, Dickens's texts move towards a dialogical structure, questioning from within the normative assumptions of their 'realistic' frames. Gothic episodes intrude throughout his novels, from *Pickwick Papers* to *Edwin Drood*, permitting a break-through of excess which then has to be recuperated as the narrative reformulates laws against transgression.

*Pickwick Papers* (1837) presents this dialogue of realistic and fantastic modes in acute form. Interpolated tales, 'The Story of the Convict's Return', 'A Madman's Manuscript',

'The Old Man's Tale about the Queer Client', etc., are different in kind from the rational discourse of Mr Pickwick's Papers. Nine stories of crime, poverty, madness, suicide, derangement, deprivation, vengeance, these tales are Gothic 'pockets of darkness' stuck into the main text. Steven Marcus sees them representing 'the obverse principle to that which informs the body of the novel. In them motion and movement of both language and event come to a dead halt. In almost every one of them . . . someone is paralysed, immobilized.' [10] Like Gaskell's fantasies of paralysis and stasis, Dickens's Gothic scenes effectively withdraw from the 'real' as it is defined by a dominant realistic tradition. Fantastic episodes resist being incorporated into the general ideological flow of his novels: their 'unreason' irrupts into and interrupts the main discourse, expressing all that has been excluded.

Dickens's subsequent novels move closer towards a fantastic idiom in presenting socially subversive energies. *Oliver Twist* (1837–9), *The Old Curiosity Shop* (1841), *Dombey and Son* (1848), employ a Gothic rhetoric to tell of parts of society held to be horrific to bourgeois security. Thieves, madmen, criminals, unmarried mothers, foreigners, prostitutes, the poor, the working class, the 'refuse' of metropolitan society, are represented through a Gothic convention as horrific, melodramatic, 'demonic', 'other'. Areas of lower-class existence are, as Dombey rejects them, 'haunts and society not to be thought of without a shudder'. Depiction of social and sexual 'otherness' as demonic, as devilish and evil, increased during the years which followed the outbreaks of European revolution in 1848. From then onwards, as Marx graphically imaged it in the opening of the *Communist Manifesto* (1848), 'A spectre is haunting Europe'. A fantastic mode had always permitted a society to write out its greatest fears as 'demonic', or 'devilish': for the Victorian middle class, these were the threats of transformation of social and sexual mores. A 'devil' was no longer even equivocally super-human: it was a working-class revolutionary, a desiring female, a social outsider or 'madman'.

Dickens's *Barnaby Rudge* (1841) turns Gordon rioters into a stereotyped mob, 'men possessed . . . like so many devils . . . a mad monster . . . the wilder and more cruel the men grew [the more] they changed their earthly nature for the qualities that give delight in hell.' 'If Bedlam gates had been flung open wide, there would not have issued forth such maniacs as the frenzy of that night made.' *The Old Curiosity Shop* depicts the Black Country as an industrialized hell and its Chartist workers as demons. *Hard Times* (1854) equates all political revolution with barbarism. *A Tale Of Two Cities* (1859) follows Carlyle's *History* by presenting the French Revolution as a grotesque plague of madness, with the Carmagnole as a vast dance of death: 'There could not be fewer than five hundred people and they were dancing like five thousand demons (. . .) some ghastly apparition of a dance figure gone raving mad rose among them'.[11]

Similar traces of a demonic idiom are present through Dickens's later work, *Little Dorrit, Our Mutual Friend, Great Expectations, Edwin Drood*, depicting a society become 'other' and persons ceasing to coincide with themselves in a metropolitan landscape. His novels are riddled with contradictions in their use of the fantastic, on the one hand alienating the reader from a 'demonic' world which lies outside bourgeois reality, but on the other locating all energy and vitality within that under-world. *The Old Curiosity Shop* sacrifices the grotesque Quilp by a traditional vampire ritual, leaving him 'to be buried with a stake in his heart in the centre of four lonely roads', but the novel runs down, losing its energy with his death. *Bleak House* hunts down the secrets hidden by the demonic figure of Lady Dedlock, who is uncannily familiar to Esther, the narrator. Lady Dedlock's concealed guilt breaks social taboos: her illicit sexuality is punished by the death of her lover Nemo (no-one) and her own melodramatic graveyard end. There is no place for her in Esther's narrative. The very title of the novel suggests Dickens's apprehension of the bleakness, the waste, the cost of sacrificing the 'demonic' for the sake of cultural order. As a fantasist, he is tempted – like Balzac – by desire without life, but as a realist, he returns to a life of repression.

Dickens relies heavily upon a Gothic tradition and provides numerous tales of doubled, inverted or partial selves.[12] *Great Expectations* realizes Pip's transgressive desires through his 'doubles', Orlick and Magwitch (desires to steal and to kill his sister), but both are encountered and 'exorcised'. Dickens's prose is 'fantastic' in its elisions, its grotesque images, its sliding from metaphor to metonymy. Nothing is stable, forms merge together, tending towards undifferentiation. The famous opening of *Bleak House* with its emphasis upon things emerging out of invisibility and amorphousness is a piece of 'fantastic realism', slowly distinguishing discrete forms and units out of a murky, indistinct mass. The city itself has become fantastic, undifferentiated, a vast inchoate mass where beings merge together and things are promiscuous, amorphous. The metropolis in Dickens's novels is a gaping mouth, a vampiric monster consuming the people who give it life. Thus in *Dombey and Son* (Chapter 33), travellers to the city are 'swallowed up in one phase or other of its immensity, towards which they seemed impelled by a desperate fascination, they never returned. Food for the hospitals, the churchyards, the prisons, the river, fever, madness, vice, and death – they passed on to the monster, roaring in the distance, and were lost.' Dickens's innumerable double and partial identities, his frequent use of synechdoche, presenting 'characters' as fragmented bodies, his mass of material objects tending to slide away from coherent structures, all indicate his development of fantasy to represent a world threatening to drift towards something 'other'. He anticipates Thomas Pynchon's fantastic narratives of 'promiscuity', of the increasing formlessness of capitalism and the fragmentation of its subjects.

Closest to Dickens's novels and heavily influenced by their fantastic realism are the writings of Dostoevsky. Like Dickens, Dosteovsky uses horrific 'underworld' material to present the crippling effects of metropolitan and industrial society upon the emotional and psychic life of the individual. Through his tales, *The Gambler, A Nasty Story, The House of the Dead, Notes from an Underground Man, The Dream of a Queer Fellow, The Double*, and his major novels, *Crime and Punishment, The Possessed, The Brothers Karamazov*, Dostoevsky develops a literature appropriate to express the strange, alienating consequences of capitalism. The main structural and semantic features which characterize the fantastic as a literary mode are present in Dostoevsky's works. As Bakhtin argues, Dostoevsky's novels are sustained dialogues, interrogating the 'normal' world and relativizing its values. His metropolis, St Petersburg (parallel to Dickens's London and to Pynchon's Washington), is un-covered to reveal a vast necropolis, a landscape of the dead and dying.

Dostoevsky effectively 'hollows out' the real world, discovering a latent emptiness. His social deviants 'sink' towards a dead world within the real one (like Mary Shelley's and Gaskell's figures, withdrawn from social engagement), implicitly protesting against a dominant order. Thus Dostoevsky's withdrawn underground man: 'The point is to understand everything, to realize everything, every impossibility, every stone wall; not to reconcile yourself to a single one of the impossibilities and stone walls if the thought of reconciliation sickens you (. . .).' [13] He believes he is responsible for the stone wall, but is unsure how: all he knows is his impotence, ignorance, aware that 'an object for your anger can't even be found', that all he has is his suffering, 'in spite of all the mysteries and illusions, you ache with it all, and the more mysterious it is, the more you ache.' He is left with withdrawal from the 'real' into an unsatisfactory 'other' unreality, feeling 'you are somehow to blame for the stone wall itself, even though once again it is abundantly clear that you are not to blame at all, and in consequence of all this to sink voluptuously into inertia, silently and impotently gnashing your teeth.' 'After all', confesses this 'imaginary' personage, 'the direct, immediate, legitimate fruit of heightened consciousness is inertia, that is, the deliberate refusal to do anything.'

Dostoevsky's protagonists are in opposition to monological definitions of the real, or of fixed personal identity. They subvert an official, public sense of reality. His Ivan Karamazov suggests (like Sade) that everything is possible if the soul is not immortal. Dostoevsky's numerous doubles, like Dickens's, draw attention to the various possible selves which are sacrificed for the sake of one's cultural identity. Through the double, 'the possibilities of another man and another life are revealed', writes Bakhtin. 'The dialogical attitude of man to himself . . . contributes to the destruction of his integrity and finalizedness' (p.96). Dostoevsky does not present 'characters', but disintegrated figures who no longer coincide with their 'ideal' selves, i.e. their culturally formed egos. *The Double* tells of Golyadkin's ideal other completely taking over his life, so that he is a mere negative image. It has already been implied that what Bakhtin terms carnivalistic and official selves can be made equivalent to Lacan's distinction between different stages of development, the imaginary and the symbolic: Dostoevsky's desire to return to the first subverts the values upheld through the second.

Dostoevsky insists upon his fidelity to 'truth': 'What other people call fantastic, I hold to be the inmost essence of truth.' Dostoevsky undermines and corrodes the heart of a public 'reality'. As with Mary Shelley, Gaskell, Dickens, Kafka or Pynchon, it would be misleading to dismiss Dostoevsky's bleakness as personal nihilism. His figures are estranged from the social, occupying a 'paraxial' realm, because they do not feel themselves to be integrated within the symbolic order. 'In Dostoevsky the participants in the performance stand *on the threshold* (the threshold of life and death, truth and falsehood, sanity and insanity) . . . "today's corpses", capable neither of dying, nor of being born anew' (Bakhtin, p.122).

Dostoevsky's short tale *Bobok* (1873) exemplifies this intermediate position. Its narrator, Ivan Ivanovich, is distanced from his own life so that the 'I' he narrates becomes a 'he'. He is drawn by a funeral procession to a graveyard where he sits on a stone, listening. When he hears voices, we are unsure whether they are supernatural (from the dead) or self-generated (originating from Ivan). The tale fulfils Todorov's first requirement of the fantastic, that it sustain ambiguity. 'And how did I happen to begin hearing different voices?' he asks. He tries to ignore them, but they are strange echoes, 'muffled, as though issuing from mouths covered with pillows.' [14] Through a dialogue with the dead, the tale effects the same misrule as a menippean tradition, annihilating social difference. Death ceases to be a definitive ending. A garrulous corpse is heard to say that 'up above, while we were still alive, we were mistaken in supposing that death there was death. The body revives again, as it were . . . It's that – I don't know how to express it – life continues by inertia.' There is no language from fully disintegrated corpses: the last sounds they utter are non-signifying syllables, 'bobok'. 'There's one person here who's almost completely decomposed, but once every six weeks or so he will suddenly mutter a word or two, quite meaningless of course, about some little bean: "Bobok, bobok".' These 'nonsense' utterances are the last differentiating signs of the human as it lapses back to an inhuman inorganicism: 'The main thing is two or three months of life and, at the very end – bobok.'

Dostoevsky's un-covering of this meaningless, entropic zone uses fantasy rather more directly as a subversive mode than it is found in Lytton, Stevenson or Wells, where it is almost immediately re-covered. He pulls the reader towards a vision of a world other than this one, an 'unreal' underground reality, between life and death, from which all cultural order seems an absurd imposition. Such estrangement is not *chosen*: it is the consequence of a dissatisfaction with the 'real' as secularized, urban, atheistic, and 'unnatural', with what the underground man terms 'our negative age'.

A 'hollowing out' of the real is viewed from another angle by three major novelists, George Eliot, Henry James and Joseph Conrad, a triad from F.R. Leavis's 'great tradition' of the English novel.[15] Their use of the double motif manifests a violent hostility towards an 'other' imaginary realm. George Eliot's tale *The Lifted Veil* (1859) makes explicit a rejection of the non-thetic. Its narrator, Latimer, insists that cultural order depends upon *not* knowing, upon keeping things obscure, concealed. 'So absolute is our soul's need of something hidden and uncertain for the maintenance of that doubt and hope and effort which are the breath of its life.'[16] Latimer has transgressed human bounds, he has seen too much. His 'microscopic vision' (like Lytton's prescient Zanoni) enables him to see through the veil, to 'all the struggling chaos', to 'the presence of something unknown and pitiless'. He has an uncanny control over events, 'causing' his brother's death. His wife's unconscious longings (to murder him) are painfully apparent: 'Horror was my familiar, and this new revelation was only like an old pain recurring with new circumstances.' He interprets his 'double consciousness' as the punishment for his desire to know, to penetrate to an absolute meaning. Discovering mere horror, he longs for ignorance, he tries to reconstruct a divine 'Unknown Presence revealed and yet hidden by the moving curtain of the earth and sky'. He wants only to return to a single, monistic vision, 'No matter how empty the adytum, so that the veil be thick enough'.

Whereas Mary Shelley, James Hogg, Gaskell, Dostoevsky, present dualism as a means of articulating feelings of estrangement, effectively subverting a social order which makes that division the condition of being, George Eliot and Henry James polemically refute anything non-thetic within their texts. Hence their movement away from a fantastic mode and their strong commitment to 'realism'. James's novels rely upon an elaborate narrative structure, both on levels of individual sentences and of plots, to distance any possibility of dissolution of 'syntax'. His hostility to the demonic is particularly clear in his tale of dualism, *The Jolly Corner* (1908).[17] Its protagonist, Spencer Brydon, returns to America from Europe after an absence of thirty years. He is drawn towards the Gothic enclosure of his old family house, where he tries to discover his long-forgotten protean selves, which were lost when he became his present self, his ego. Brydon seeks his 'alter ego', 'the form he so yearned to make [his old possibilities] take'. He half fears, half desires to meet his double, the imaginary presence which is more like an absence, figuring all that he has *not* been. Compelled further inwards, to the centre of the empty mansion, Brydon is faced with a moment of crisis, when he has to choose whether or not to open the door which separates self from other. At this critical juncture, analogous to George Eliot's metaphorical 'lifting of the veil' (or to a metaphorical process of walking backwards through the mirror to an Imaginary Other), Brydon selects *not* to know. 'He wouldn't touch it – it seemed now that he might if he would: he would only just wait there a little, to show, to prove, that he wouldn't.' In the name of 'Discretion', he retreats from the closed door.

His spectral 'other', however, waits upon him, blocking his exit from the family home. It is less a supernatural emanation than a figure through which Brydon's hidden self is revealed to him. It provokes pure 'Horror (. . .) for the bared identity was too hideous as *his*.'

> The penumbra, dense and dark, was the virtual screen of a figure which stood in it. . . . He saw, in its great grey glimmering margin, the central vagueness diminish, and he felt it to be taking the very form toward which . . . the passion of his curiosity had yearned. It gloomed, it loomed, it was something, it was somebody, the prodigy of a personal presence.
>
> Rigid and conscious, spectral yet human, a man of his

own substance and stature waited there to measure himself with his power to dismay. (pp.342–3)

Brydon looks away 'in dismay and denial'. He retreats from the horror of this fluid, multiple other, and reconstructs his familiar 'ego', which is directly opposed to the 'evil, odious, blatant (and) vulgar' sides which it conceals.

> It was unknown, inconceivable, awful, disconnected from any possibility . . . Such an identity fitted his at *no* point, made its alternative monstrous . . . the face was the face of a stranger . . . [like] one of those expanding images projected by the magic lantern of childhood; for the stranger, whoever he might be, evil, odious, blatant, vulgar, had advanced as for aggression . . . (p.344)

Like George Eliot, James pushes away that which is read as 'evil, odious, vulgar' to the margins of a 'realistic' discourse, where it remains a mute, spectral presence.

Joseph Conrad's fantasy of the double, *The Secret Sharer* (1913), re-works problems of demonic encounter told in *The Heart of Darkness* (1902) and has a resolution which aligns him with Eliot and James. Like *The Jolly Corner*, this fantasy presents a direct confrontation of self and other. A ghostly side suddenly materializes on a sea voyage, summoned by the narrator's doubt as to his ability to 'be' his ideal ego. 'I wondered how far I should turn out faithful to that ideal conception of one's own personality every man sets up for himself secretly.'[18] His second self comes on board, is concealed for several days and a mysterious communication is established, in whispers, between them. No one else perceives it, so uncertainty arises as to the substance of the sharer. The double is a long forgotten 'other' side, 'Like something against nature, inhuman'. It has committed a murder, and for several days it is concealed, so that their complicity is recognized. 'It was, in the night, as though I had been faced by my own reflection in the depths of a sombre and immense mirror.' As with previous fantasies of dualism, the two sides are not reconciled. The 'other' reminds 'self', ' "It would never do for me to come to life again . . . You must maroon me as soon as ever you can . . . there's nothing else for it." ' It is 'driven off the face of the earth', abandoned near some waste islands in a permanent exile, 'to be hidden forever'. Conrad presents this severance as a proper resolution, as 'self' renounces his libidinal other and assumes an adult life. The imaginary is relinquished with little regret.

A self-conscious confrontation of humanism with something *on the edge*, something beyond, or before, or outside human culture, takes very different forms through the works of George Eliot, James and Conrad from its appearance in Dickens, Dostoevsky, Balzac, or more extreme fantasists. Narrative positioning as regards the 'double' makes this clear: *The Lifted Veil, The Jolly Corner, The Secret Sharer*, are all narrated by a 'self' who finally represses his latent other and restores a familiar identity, no matter what is excluded. *The Underground Man, The Double* (and even, to some extent, *A Tale of Two Cities*) are from the 'other's' side: they are told as if from the phantom selves lost during the construction of a more substantial, unified 'character', and so they can provide a disturbing, subversive account of what is lost through the process of cultural formation. A tradition of humanism, by contrast, dismisses the demonic as 'evil, odious, blatant, vulgar', reading all otherness as mere barbarism, thus reinforcing solid boundaries against the 'fantastic' and 'unreal'.

# 6 VICTORIAN FANTASIES

Life slips away and life on the other side of the great river becomes more and more the reality, of which *this* is only a shadow.

Lewis Carroll

THE more popular Victorian fantasists, Lewis Carroll, George MacDonald, Charles Kingsley, reveal an attraction towards that 'zero' point of undifferentiation and inorganicism which characterizes fantasy, but with a strong repudiation of its a-moral, barbaric elements. Carroll's writings are the most clearly 'fantastic'. They draw attention to problems of signification, presenting a confused, topsy-turvy world which lays no claim to re-present absolute meaning or 'reality'. When Alice falls down the rabbit hole and walks through the mirror in *Alice in Wonderland* (1865) and *Through the Looking-Glass* (1872), she enters a realm of non-signification, of non-sense. She is faced with semiotic chaos, and her acquired language systems cease to be of any help. Things slip away from words – a baby becomes a pig, a grin becomes a cat – and words assume lives of their own, 'the phrase insisted on conjugating itself'. 'No word', writes Carroll, 'has a meaning inseparably attached to it.' For Carroll, as for Wittgenstein, language is the means of constructing meaning – outside a language world, there lies only non-meaning.[1]

Deprived of habitual linguistic codes, Alice is faced with the end of the world as she knows it. Her ontological insecurity seems to have more to do with this deprivation of signs which mean, than with the grotesque, grinning, apparently cruel underworld of monsters, caucuses, caterpillars, pigs, executioners, or tormenters, into which she falls. What worries her most is a loss of identity: all she can hang on to is her name, yet she doesn't know what it means. She is threatened with an immanent loss of meaning, for without language there is no differentiation of self from other. ' "Who are *you*?" said the Caterpillar. "I . . . hardly know . . . I can't explain *myself* . . . because I'm not myself", replied Alice. "You know very well you're not real", said Tweedledum and Tweedledee. "I *am* real!" said Alice, and began to cry.' Humpty Dumpty reproaches her, 'You *should* have meant. . . . What do you suppose is the use of a child without any meaning?' Humpty Dumpty has been termed 'the master of the signifier' (Lacan, *The Language of Self*, p.57) playing with interchangeable signs and words. Alice is the victim of this game, another pawn, but neither of them has the key to the puzzle's meaning. That kind of 'semiotic excess' which comes to predominate in modernist fiction has its roots in Carroll's play with signs deprived of significance.

For all their ludic qualities, the *Alice* books are neither particularly funny, nor joyful. The Queen tells Alice, 'I wish I could manage to be glad! Only I can never remember the rule.' Their hollowness stems from their negation of meaning. There are no ends, only signs which lead nowhere, landscapes which are labyrinths without a centre. 'She found herself in a long, low hall. . . . There were doors all round the hall, but they were all locked.' She was 'wandering up and down, and trying turn after turn, but always coming back.' Guides give her the wrong directions and her futile quests bring her back to her starting point, as she moves forward merely to stay still. ' "Now, *here*, you see," ' the Queen tells her, ' "it takes all the running you can do, to keep in the same place. If you want to get somewhere else, you must run at least twice as fast as that." ' Effects precede their causes: a piece of cake is eaten, then cut. The text multiplies incertitude, no definite position can be taken, no definitive meaning is established. A sign can mean anything.

Various psychoanalytic interpretations have read Alice's nightmare of not meaning as a fear of losing control, of becoming a body which has no stable identity.[2] She fears losing herself by becoming another. She is obsessed with physical changes effected by eating, drinking, laughing, crying, dancing, entering, leaving. Her human body becomes a 'thing', an object which shrinks, extends, transforms from one dimension to another. Alice longs for a fixed shape: her quest is to return to her original 'known' self, for she is divorced from her body, protected from time and from social relations, terrified of *change*. Empson sees this as a fear of sexuality and of death: the consequences of accepting the 'body' as self (Empson, p.227).

Elizabeth Sewell provides a similar (though non-sexual) reading of Carroll's work in *The Field of Nonsense* (1952), one of the first critical studies of Carroll and Lear. Sewell interprets Carroll's retreat from undifferentiation as produced by a fear of 'love' as something unitive, open, anti-logical: 'love', or 'desire', threatens Carroll's logical world with dissolution. Towards the end of *Through the Looking-Glass*, Alice walks through 'a wood, much darker than the last wood', where things have no names. In this darkness, she experiences a transitory moment of joy, as she embraces (loves) a Faun, but their brief encounter comes to an end as soon as they leave the wood and re-enter the linguistic field. A place without words is Carroll's image of joy, but he cannot reach it: he returns to the empty pleasures of signs and language games. Sewell makes some important distinctions between nonsense and a more magical type of fantasy, which relate to this different attitude towards language.

Nonsense, she writes, 'engages the force towards disorder in continual play.' It tends to re-combine different semantic units which remain distinct from one another. It fractures rather than dissolves, returning to rigidity and a separation of individual units. Stephen Prickett writes similarly, that 'Far from being "free" or formless, it [nonsense] is the most highly organized and the most rigidly controlled of all forms of fantasy (Prickett, p.126). It is a fantasy of extreme logic, of rationality pushed to its limits. It was this controlled literary fantasy which became so popular amongst a Victorian middle class. The publication of Edward Lear's *Book of Nonsense* (1846) established nonsense as a minor genre, with his limericks, comic verse and riddles surviving through Carroll and his puns to Mervyn Peake's *Rhymes without Reason*. This nonsense is a literature of semantic play, juggling with incongruous relations between possible units. These are not fantasies according to Todorov's scheme, for they provoke no ambiguity of response in the reader. They are 'legalized' by various framing devices such as the mirror, or a chess game, or a dream wonderland: self-contained realms which are neutralized and distanced through a manifestly impossible frame.

Less well-known than the *Alice* books, yet closer to fantasy than nonsense literature, are Carroll's poems, *Phantasmagoria* (1869), *The Hunting of the Snark* (1876) and his two-volumed *Sylvie and Bruno* (1889). *Snark* has a topography without signification. It is imprecise, vacant, without boundaries or features. A map of it is 'A perfect and absolute blank'. The poem revolves around the baker's terror of the Snark, yet we never know what the Snark (really a 'Boojum') *is*. A thing without a signifier and a signifier without an object, this 'Boojum' cannot be represented directly in the poem. It has 'swallowed up' the baker: 'He had softly and suddenly vanished away.' Yet to allegorize the Snark as death would be to impose a reductive conceptualizing scheme which the poem internally resists, as it moves towards an indefinite ending, without 'meaning'.

*Sylvie and Bruno* intensifies a shift towards the fantastic, especially during its opening scenes. Carroll's *Preface* admits that this work, more than any other, had given him 'a far clearer idea . . . of the meaning of the word "chaos" '. It kaleidoscopes 'real' and 'faery' events, producing 'eerie', 'uncanny' effects (the narrator's words). A minimally linear narrative is fragmented by sudden intrusions of song, laughter, dance, dream, where things undergo metamorphosis. A mad Gardener, suddenly breaking into song, has 'the feet of an Elephant' and wisps of straw 'suggested that he had originally been stuffed with it', whilst 'even his utterances had taken on themselves a strange and dreamlike form'.

There are two 'narratives' superimposed or 'imbricated' upon one another in *Sylvie and Bruno*, making it impossible to distinguish what is seen by the narrator and what is imagined. Two women (whom the narrator secretly desires), Sylvie and Lady Muriel, are linked together through his perceptions, forming an uncanny identity. But the tale is recuperated as a pedagogic piece of children's literature, padded out with advice, instruction and moral asides. *Sylvie and Bruno* develops into a tedious, didactic tract, the kind of teaching material which Mrs Trimmer and innumerable religious writers had been advocating throughout Victoria's reign.

Carroll's pull towards a metaphysical 'meaning' at the ends of the Alice books and *Sylvie and Bruno*, seeing life as a mere dream (hence the epigraph to this chapter), aligns him with more conspicuous religious fantasists, such as George MacDonald, Charles Kingsley and, later, E. Nesbit. Victorian fantasy was heavily influenced by a tradition of Christian Platonism, which read the 'real' as the place where transcendental truths were reflected. Lapses into a non-signifying world were accordingly restrained. Thomas Carlyle's *Sartor Resartus* (1831) declared Fantasy to be 'the true Heaven and Hell gate of man', for it opened on to the infinite, through an understanding of man's finite nature.

'Fantasy is the organ of the Godlike ... Man thereby, though based to all seeming, on the small Visible, does nevertheless extend down into the infinite deeper of the Invisible, of which Invisible, indeed, his life is properly the bodying forth.'[3] It was a fallen form of imagination, a secular equivalent to great religious myths.

Stephen Prickett has traced this line of Victorian fantasy from Coleridge's famous distinction between Imagination and Fancy in *Biographia Literaria*: fantasy comes to be the profane mirror image of sacred products of imagination. Whereas *Imagination* was 'a repetition in the finite mind of the eternal act of creation in the infinite I AM', *Fancy*, or *fantasy*, is merely human, a combination of elements, re-combined into strange, unfamiliar forms.

In practice, however, mainstream Victorian fantasy is close to Coleridge's notion of Imagination. Prickett discerns a continuous line of Platonic idealism sustained through the works of Carroll, MacDonald, Kingsley, Morris, Kipling, E. Nesbit, defining their fantasies in terms of their transcendentalism. They all manifest 'a desire for something *more*,' for a 'magic city' or a visionary dream land. This is analogous, argues Prickett, to that vision of Paradise which consummates Dante's *Divine Comedy*, as an image of the cosmic harmony towards which the whole creation moves. Although 'lesser' forms than Dante's, Victorian fantasies devoutly wish for a similar consummation. It is this 'that transforms fantasy from simple escapism into something much more enduringly rooted in the human psyche' (p.235).

But it is possible to see contradictions within the writings of MacDonald and Kingsley, which suggest that their embrace of Platonic idealism was less of a transcendental movement, and more of a displacement of psychological and social issues, for their fantasies betray a dissatisfaction with their own idealism. This is particularly so with George MacDonald's work. MacDonald wrote many theological novels: *David Elginbrod* (1863), *Alec Forbes of Howglen* (1865),

*Robert Falconer* (1868), for example; some children's books: *The Golden Key* (1867), *At the Back of the North Wind* (1871), *The Princess and the Goblin* (1872), *The Princess and Curdie* (1883); and two fantasies for adults, *Phantastes* (1858) and *Lilith* (1895). They were influenced by German Romanticism, especially by Novalis, and they construct a 'dream' world, but one which is never entirely satisfactory.

*Phantastes*, 'A Faerie Romance for men and women', is told as a distant dream, insufficiently incongruous to really disturb the reader. Yet it has several qualities of a fantastic mode. Its hero, Anodos (Greek for 'the way upwards'), discovers his room inexplicably transformed into a woodland scene. It becomes peculiarly quite, without life or noise. 'I was struck with utter stillness. No bird sang. No insect hummed. Not a living creature crossed my way.' Entering the wood, Anodos comes to 'the house of the ogre', where he opens a forbidden cupboard, to discover it has no back (C.S. Lewis was to imitate this device in *The Lion, the Witch and the Wardrobe*, but as a magical device, lacking MacDonald's uneasy psychological effect of the discovery). Anodos is staring into an infinite void, a place with no shape or name, until he sees (projects) there a figure which he reads as signifying his own death:

> as I looked, I saw . . . that an empty space went in further . . . as I continued looking . . . my eyes came into true relation with their object. All at once, with such a shiver as when one is suddenly conscious of the presence of another in a room where he has, for hours, considered himself alone [I saw] a dark figure [which] sped into and along the passage . . . I started back and shuddered, but kept looking, for I could not help it . . .[4]

Anodos names this dark figure 'an evil demon'. The narrative focuses upon its exorcism, producing a magical romance of (supernatural) good against evil. Yet these early scenes suggest that Anodos is facing his double in that dark recess, similar to Brydon's encounter in James's *Jolly Corner*, or Stevenson's Jekyll mirrored by Hyde. MacDonald's fantasy *begins* as psychological projection, as an uncanny tale, and only later is developed into a moral allegory. Initially, the 'other' is beyond good or evil: it is self *as* other, as its own death. 'The strangest figure; vague, shadowy, almost transparent (. . .) the face reminded me of what I had heard of vampires; for the face resembled that of a corpse.' Its eyes 'were alive, yet not with life. They seemed lighted up with an infinite greed. A gnawing voracity, which devoured the devourer, seemed to be the indwelling and propelling power of the whole ghastly apparition.'

*Lilith* repeats this fantasy of a rehearsal with death. (Most fantasies of a 'double' or 'devil' can be interpreted as the self rehearsing his/her own death, own absence.) Its narcissistic hero, Vane, ceases to feel 'at home' in the world. His room changes into a wood and he experiences objects and people as distanced, alienated. Parallel to Dostoevsky's and Kafka's re-presentations of the real, MacDonald's hollows out the familiar world. Vane's ordinary home is dis-covered to be a house of the dead. He perceives it as hiding something strange:

> Could it be that I was dead . . . and did not know it? Was I in what we used to call the world beyond the grave? and must I wander about seeking my place in it? How was I to find myself at home?

He moves into a mirror world, then returns from it, but even on this side, he does not feel secure. The 'real' can lapse towards the 'unreal':

> I turned, and there was the mirror, on whose top the black eagle seemed but that moment to have perched. Terror seized me, and I fled. Outside the chamber the wide garret spaces had an *uncanny* look. They seemed to have long been waiting for something; it had come, and they were waiting again! A shudder went through me on the winding stair: the house had grown strange to me!

Something was about to leap upon me from behind! . . .
On the next floor I lost my way . . . I was nowhere safe!
. . . I would sell the dreadful place, in which an aerial
portal stood ever open to creatures whose life was other
than human! (pp.197–8)

Throughout *Lilith*, a topography of labyrinthine passages, wasteland, doors opening to emptiness, graveyards,
mirrors, constitutes the internal 'space' which Vane
occupies. It is a dead landscape, inhabited by ravens, eagles,
black cats, ghosts, the un-dead. 'Everywhere was the same as
*nowhere*! I had not yet, by doing something, made *anywhere*
into a place.' As his name suggests, Vane's world is
inseparable from his self-absorption. Like Dorian Gray, he
is trapped by his narcissism. 'I was not yet alive; I was only
dreaming I lived.' 'I saw that man alone is but a being that
may become a man.' 'I regarded with wonder my past self
[neglecting] the company of man or woman.' 'I had chosen
the dead rather than the living.' Yet MacDonald's tale of
movement away from this 'paraxial' realm, as a place for a
kind of death-in-life, is one which replaces one unreality for
another.

As with *Phantastes*, *Lilith* develops into a magical narrative:
its 'death-in-life' is projected on to the 'evil' figure of Lilith
from whom sterility has been supposed to derive. According
to Assyrian mythology, Lilith precedes Eve, and is produced
not from Adam's rib, but simultaneously, from the dust of
the earth, generated as an equal.[5] Lilith refuses a passive
maternal role and is cast into hell, becoming the figure
behind female succubi and vampires through many folk
legends. MacDonald reawakens this tradition by making of
Lilith a protean evil shape, 'indestructible evil, the heart of
horror essential', manifesting herself as leopardess, leech,
vampire, bat, owl, demon. On to Lilith are placed all Vane's
life-denying instincts. She becomes a malign cosmic force
operating against goodness and vitality. 'Something was
gone from her.' 'The source of life had withdrawn itself.' 'I
saw the face of a live death.'

> She knew life only to know that it was dead, and that in her, death lived. It was not merely that life had ceased in her, but that she was consciously a dead thing . . . She had tried to unmake herself . . . she was a dead life . . . existent Nothing [was] her inheritance!

By destroying Lilith, the romance moves towards an assertion of cosmic goodness, where evil is no more. 'There is a light that lightens the darkness . . .' Vane does achieve a reflection of Dante's paradisical vision, 'Love possessed me! Love was my life! Love was . . . all in all! . . . The world and its being, its life and mine, were one. The microcosm and macrocosm were at length atoned, at length in harmony. I lived in everything; everything entered and lived in me,' but it is no resolution of his narcissism. Instead of concentrating upon himself, he transfers his love to the cosmos internalized, asserting a magical faith in goodness, as some transcendental entity. MacDonald's fantasies betray dissatisfaction with the real and seek something other. They fill emptiness with a magical, divine plenitude. Yet a strange melancholy remains, as his hollow characters arrive at their ideal visions. Their ideals lie beyond the mirror, or through the north wind, in a landscape of death.

*Phantastes* and *Lilith* are not dissimilar to *Dracula* and *The Lair of the White Worm* in their ideological effects. An apprehension of something *without* signification is rewritten as 'evil' and into that evil category are exiled forms of social deviancy and subversion. Here, again, it is woman, under the sign of Lilith: woman as threat, as a demanding, desiring, angry and violent presence. MacDonald's other tales also equate female sexuality with immorality. His story *The Princess and Curdie* (1877) repeats a frequent post-Darwinian fantasy of regression to bestiality. Several characters are incompletely human: their hands have retained animal features, as the paws of a bear, claws of a dragon, scales of a snake and scorpion. The most notable monster is Lina, 'a woman that was naughty', a hybrid of dog, snake, dragon and bear.

Perhaps the most popular Victorian fantasy of this 'faery' tradition is Charles Kingsley's *The Water Babies* (1863), sub-titled 'A Fairy Tale for a Land-Baby'. Kingsley was an eminent Victorian. He was rector at Eversley, Hampshire and he received royal patronage after a sermon at Buckingham Palace in 1859. He wrote numerous theological and didactic tracts, his only piece of sustained fantasy (apart from a surrealistic sequence called 'Dreamland', Chapter 36 of his novel *Alton Locke*) being *The Water Babies*. His fiction and non-fiction were written from a determinedly anti-revolutionary position. He called himself 'the veriest aristocrat, full of hatred and contempt for those dangerous [working] classes'. *Alton Locke* describes Chartists as 'wicked and insane'. Minor street riots of Bristol had confirmed his sense of class superiority, and Carlyle's fanatical writings ('half religious, half fascistic')[6] had consolidated this position and encouraged stalwart patriotism and racism. Aborigines were 'wretched black people,' types of 'original sin', and physical deformity or infirmity was read as moral degeneration.

These prejudices are written into *The Water Babies*. It is usually published in an expurgated edition, minimizing its didacticism, but even so it is a classic text of repression, obsessed with the removal of dirt. Its first desire is for cleanliness. Mother Carey counsels Tom: 'Those that wish to be clean, clean they will be; and those that wish to be foul, foul they will be. Remember.' Tom delivers constant self-admonitions of the same kind. 'I must be clean, I must be clean.' 'Tom longed to go and see the sea, and bathe in it.' He seeks to be 'undefiled'. Behind this tedious allegory, there are similarities between Tom's quest for union with the sea and quest for undifferentiation found in other fantasies. Lautréamont's Maldoror longs for union with the ocean, always at one with itself. Sade's libertines long to be amphibious, to combine with every species. Kingsley's Tom wants to be a water baby, a four-inch sea creature, an amphibian. The desire is the same, though its Victorian form is rather different. 'Tom was amphibious: and what is better still, he was clean . . . he felt how comfortable it was to have nothing on him but himself.'[7]

C.N. Manlove's thorough discussion of *The Water Babies* identifies its impulse towards 'vigorous fantasy'. It has an 'empirical aesthetic,' a 'dynamic of process' (Manlove, pp.29–30). Long catalogues of natural forms, at random, in 'prodigal variety', celebrate natural profusion, Rabelaisian in their delight (Rabelais was one of Kingsley's favourite authors). There is a shift from animal to vegetable to mineral, a rich polymorphousness, beneath the surface. Tom's visit to the Island of Polupragmosyne, for example, at 'the Other-end-of Nowhere', where everything happens in reverse: 'Ploughs drawing horses, nails driving hammers, birds' nests taking boys . . . monkeys shaving cats'. St Brandon's, a version of Plato's Atlantis, is full of strange plants, stones, caves, and 'thousands and thousands of water-snakes . . . dressed in green velvet, and black velvet, and purple velvet'. Everything is in a state of flux, and delightful transformation: 'he saw . . . water-monkeys and water-squirrels . . . water-flowers [which] as soon as he touched them . . . drew themselves in and turned into knots of jelly . . . all alive – bells, and stars, and wheels, and flowers, of all beautiful shapes and colours.'[8]

This natural disorder implies to Kingsley 'the unrestrained and amorally healthy' (Manlove, p.34). Not surprisingly, it is written out as an allegory, for it cannot be reconciled with demands for control and moral unity. 'Matter' can be justified in this context only as a sign of divine presence. On his marriage to Fanny Grenfell (1844), Kingsley had referred to matter as 'holy, awful, glorious'. 'Our animal enjoyments must be religious ceremonies', thereby 'making of the debauchee a preacher of purity and holiness, and of the destroyer of systems a weak though determined upholder of the only true system.' A delight in physicality is repressed, to serve divine ends, and Kingsley's fantasy is to discover 'a divine element underlying all physical nature'.

Why this prodigal variety? . . . What a waste of power, on any utilitarian theory of nature! . . . Inexplicable, truly, if man be the centre and the object of their existence . . . if we come to *find* causes, there is no better answer than the old mystic one, that God has imprest the law of *Love* on matter, that it may be a type of the spiritual world when healthy, and of the Kingdom of Heaven. (cit. Manlove, p.34)

The result, for Kingsley's narrative, is a re-working of fantastic elements into Christian theology, under the guise of 'fairy tale'. But Kingsley's faith in 'a good time coming', his 'absolute certainty of resurrection' excludes from salvation all impure souls unworthy of redemption – such unregenerates as blacks, Catholics, and a revolutionary working class. The ideological implications of this hardly need spelling out. Behind chimneysweep Tom's obsessive desire 'to be clean' is a desire to rise in class status, and to be rewarded with an ideal of unity and perfection as embodied by a white, English, aristocratic, 'beautiful', 'pure', maiden: rich Ellie, daughter of the local landowner at Harthover House: Ellie as the new Beatrice to Tom's Dante.

The creations of Carroll, MacDonald, Kingsley, Machen, Nesbit, de la Mare, Kipling, Morris, etc. have been called ' "the high fantasy" of a world too rich and complex to be contained by the conventions of Victorian naturalism' (Prickett, p.235). Yet this metaphor of height betrays the critic's transcendentalism. Twentieth-century romancers and critics have sustained these Victorian fantasists' repressive creations. J.R.R. Tolkien's theoretical essay on faery literature echoes MacDonald and Kingsley, for it advocates that function as a lesser version of religious myths, re-working the redemptive story of Christ's death and resurrection. 'Faery' leads to 'the Consolation of the Happy Ending', which Tolkien calls Eucatastrophe. 'The eucatastrophic tale is the true form of the fairy-tale, and its highest function.' Its joy and consolation is a form of grace, denying defeat, hoping to provide 'a fleeting glimpse of Joy, Joy beyond the walls of the world' (Tolkien, *Tree and Leaf*, p.60).

Tolkien's Middle-earth of *The Lord of the Rings*, like Morris's land in his romance, *The Wood Beyond the World* and MacDonald's paradise of *The Golden Key*, is outside the human. An imagined realm with its own order, it is free from the demands of historical time, or of mortality. Tolkien sees the function of faery as three-fold: to provide recovery, escape and consolation; it promises wish fulfilment, magical satisfaction. Theorists of fairy tales all stress this consolatory function of the marvellous. 'The fairy tale is the poetic expression of the confidence that we are secure in a world not destitute of sense' (Lüthi, p.145). 'The fairy tale is not about ordinary people . . . the participants and events take place in another atmosphere,' (Franz, p.6). As narrative forms, fairy tales function differently from fantasies. They are neutral, impersonalized, set apart from the reader. The reader becomes a passive receiver of events, there is no demand that (s)he participate in their interpretation. *Structurally, too, fairy tales discourage belief in the importance or effectiveness of action* for their narratives are 'closed'. Things 'happen', 'are done *to*' protagonists, told *to* the reader, from a position of omniscience and authority, making the reader unquestioningly passive.

Modern 'faery' literature operates similarly to the quasi-religious works of MacDonald and Kingsley. Ursula Le Guin's recent science fantasies, which she calls 'psychomyths', provide a promise of redemption on cosmic and personal levels. As in romance tales, a dark 'other' in her *Earthsea* trilogy is magically defeated. *The City of Illusions* unites two heroes, Falk and Ramarren, into one man. *The Left Hand of Darkness* synthesizes male and female, light and darkness, life and death, upon the planet of Winter. These miraculous unities are myths of psychic order which help to contain critiques of disorder. Their utopianism does not directly engage with divisions or contradictions of subjects *inside* human culture: their harmony is established on a mystical cosmic level.[9] C.S. Lewis's *Perelandra* trilogy, his

Christian parable, *The Lion, the Witch and the Wardrobe*, T.H. White's medieval romances such as *The Once and Future King*, Stephen Donaldson's imitative 'Tolkien' trilogy, *Lord Foul's Bane*, *The Illearth War*, *The Power that Preserves*, are all of the same kind, functioning as conservative vehicles for social and instinctual repression.

Whereas fantasies (of dualism) by Mary Shelley, Dickens, Stevenson, etc., interrogate the cost of constructing an ego, thereby challenging the very formation of a symbolic cultural order, romances (of integration) by Le Guin, Lewis, White, etc., leave problems of social order untouched. Dickens, Dostoevsky and Kafka create a space where a turning of the 'right' hand into the 'left' might be effected, but Le Guin, etc., insist that right and left are synthesized, are as one. Besides their difference in redeploying the motif of the double, another telling thematic difference is their use of anthropomorphism. *Jekyll and Hyde*, *Dracula*, or Kafka's *Metamorphosis* dis-cover bestial elements within the human: what had been assumed to be known is horribly alien. Less disturbing 'faery' tales work oppositely, imposing human characteristics upon an animal kingdom. From Walter de la Mare, Beatrix Potter, A.A. Milne, to Richard Adams and J.R.R. Tolkien, a tradition of liberal humanism spreads outwards, covering with its moral, social, and linguistic orthodoxies a world of bears, foxes, wolves, rabbits, ducks, hens and hobbits. George Orwell's *Animal Farm* usefully translates animal into man for purposes of political allegory, but these romantic fables are more sentimental and nostalgic. They reinforce a blind faith in 'eternal' moral values, really those of an outworn liberal humanism.

The current popularity of J.R.R. Tolkien's *The Hobbit* and *The Lord of the Rings* indicates the strength of a romance tradition supporting a ruling ideology. Tolkien is nostalgic for a pre-Industrial, indeed a pre-Norman Conquest, feudal order. He makes a naive equation of industry with evil, referring with disgust to the 'materialism of a Robot Age' and looking backwards to a medieval paradise, his secondary worlds providing coherence and unity. An Oxford professor of philology, Tolkien allies morality and aesthetics: virtue lies with a beautiful Elvish Speech, evil with an ugly Black Speech. Whereas English literature stops with D.H. Lawrence in F.R. Leavis's canon, it ceases with Chaucer in Tolkien's, apart from a few of William Morris's romances. For Tolkien, the only way is backwards: the chauvinistic, totalitarian effects of his vision are conveniently removed from present material conditions, by providing an 'escape' from them. He is repelled (like Carroll) by the physical and material. Tolkien's Orcs, the dark hairy creatures of *The Lord of the Rings*, are imaged as repulsively sensual, as embodiments of absolute evil, whereas for Blake they are the instruments of revolution.[10]

Behind the 'high' fantasy of Kingsley, MacDonald, Morris, Tolkien, Lewis, etc., there is a recognizable 'death wish', which has been identified as one recurrent feature of fantasy literature. Whereas more subversive texts activate a dialogue with this death drive, directing their energy towards a dissolution of repressive structures, these more conservative fantasies simply go along with a desire to cease 'to be', a longing to transcend or escape the human. They avoid the difficulties of confrontation, that tension between the imaginary and the symbolic which is the crucial, problematic area dramatized in more radical fantasies.

# 7 FROM KAFKA'S 'METAMORPHOSIS' TO PYNCHON'S 'ENTROPY'

Every word that evokes the idea of the other side, of metamorphosis ... is to be welcomed here as being exactly appropriate.

Thomas Mann, *Doctor Faustus*

CONTRASTED with the 'faery' literature of J.R.R. Tolkien, C.S. Lewis and T.H. White, is a line of twentieth-century works continuing a fantastic tradition as it had developed from Gothic through Dickens, Poe, Dostoevsky, Stevenson, etc. Dostoevsky's apprehension of another 'language', a 'latent, as yet unspoken future Word', finds a strange realization in the fantastic *as* a language in Kafka, Cortázar, Gracq, Peake and Pynchon. As Sartre identifies it, this language of difference is not new, but is a long familiar discourse. It has now 'become what it always had been': a discourse telling of absolute otherness.

Various semantic transformations of literary fantasy from the late eighteenth to the late nineteenth century have been explained by shifts in ideas and beliefs. A gradual displacement of residual supernaturalism and magic, an increasingly secularized mode of thought under capitalism, produced radical changes in interpretations and presentations of otherness, i.e. of the demonic, with which fantasy has traditionally concerned itself. These shifts record a move away from orthodox demonology towards psychology, to account for difference and strangeness. Literary fantasies from *The Castle of Otranto* to *Jekyll and Hyde* are determined by these transitions: from conventional diabolism in Beckford's *Vathek*, through the equivocations of *Frankenstein*, *Melmoth* and *The Confessions of a Justified Sinner*, to the internalized figures of *Dorian Gray* or the self-generated 'ghosts' of *The Turn of the Screw* and *The Jolly Corner*.

In this perspective, theology and psychology function in similar ways, to explain otherness. They have become substitutions for the sacred, or, as Jameson writes, strategic secular re-inventions of it. Fantasy shifts from one 'explanation' of otherness to another in the course of its history. It moves from supernaturalism and magic to theology and science to categorize or define otherness. Freud's theories of the Unconscious are one means of explaining, or rationalizing, this realm. As Jameson suggests, these categorizations become strangely redundant from the late nineteenth century onwards – what he terms 'the new positivities' no longer suffice:

> the search for secular equivalents of this kind seems to have reached a dead end, and to be replaced by the new and characteristic indirection of modernism, which, in what from Kafka to Cortázar is henceforth termed the 'fantastic', seeks to convey the sacred, not as a presence, but rather as a determinate, marked absence at the heart of the secular world. (Jameson, p.145)

Fantasies express a longing for an absolute meaning, for something other than the limited 'known' world. Yet whereas 'faery' stories and quasi-religious tales function through nostalgia for the sacred, the modern fantastic refuses a backward-looking glance. It is an inverted form of myth. It focuses upon the unknown within the present, discovering emptiness inside an apparently full reality.

Absence itself is foregrounded, placed at the semantic centre of the text. The modern fantastic, writes Jameson, presents 'an object world forever suspended on the point of meaning, forever disposed to receive a revelation, whether of evil or of grace, that never takes place' (p.146).

A powerful myth of endlessly unsatisfied desire becomes one of the hallmarks of modernism. Geoffrey Hartmann's  article, 'The fullness and nothingness of literature', sees modern literature as characterized by its preoccupation with silences, absences, lacks of meaning, whilst Ihab Hassan's *The Dismemberment of Orpheus* describes modernism as pulled towards a condition of silence, of non-being. Like the tramps Vladimir and Estragon in Beckett's *Waiting for Godot*, modern fiction is waiting, interminably, for an impossible epiphany (defined by Joyce as a 'sudden spiritual manifestation'). Absolute signification never arrives, yet the possibility of its appearance cannot be ruled out. Religious or spiritual epiphany becomes inconceivable: matter is merely matter, unredeemed, yet strangely hollowed out, insufficient in itself. Without meaning, without transcendence, modern fantasy still functions as if meaning and transcendence were to be found. It uncovers mere absence and emptiness, yet it continues its quest for an absolute. Waiting, impossible expectation, *l'attente*, are characteristics of modern fiction, from Kafka to Beckett and Pynchon. As Cortázar writes, 'nothing is missing, not even, and especially, nothingness, the true solidifier of the scene.' [1]

Franz Kafka's writings reveal many of the qualities which have been identified as belonging to a fantastic mode. His historical situation pushed him towards fantasy as an appropriate form for expressing social estrangement. Kafka's tales and unfinished novels are 'fantastic' at a level beyond the marvellous or the uncanny. Their extraordinary actuality cannot be located as supernatural or as generated by a misapprehending subject. Strangeness is taken as a given, before the narrative begins: it is the inevitable condition of being, apprehended as an external disorder which the text tries to reproduce and comprehend.

Kafka's *Metamorphosis* (1916) images a lapse from human to inhuman, parallel to the transformations of *Frankenstein* and *Jekyll and Hyde*. Gregor Samsa's change from man to giant beetle, though, does not occur through marvellous intervention (supernaturalism, magic, quasi-scientific experiments or potions) or through unconscious motivation (uncannily revealing a latent desire). It is a transformation without cause. It precedes the start of the tale, without Gregor's will. It can be read, like Gaskell's *The Grey Woman* or *Six Weeks at Heppenheim*, as a movement from self to other in protest against an oppressive reality, progressively withdrawing from a culture's 'humanizing' schemes. Questions of 'how' or 'why' are not relevant: the text deflects metaphorical conceptualizations. There is no 'meaning' to Gregor's transformation. It simply operates upon him, converting his human organism into so much waste matter, pulling him towards entropy.

Gregor Samsa's movement from life to death is painfully transcribed. His body is no longer 'his'. His room ceases to be 'homely': it is 'a naked den' for his senseless crawling. Objects are removed, the walls made naked. 'The lofty, empty room in which he had to lie flat on the floor filled him with an apprehension he could not account for.' [2] He loses his sight, forgets identities, gradually sheds all memory of his origins, 'all recollection of his human background', perceiving from his window only 'a desert waste where grey sky and grey land blended indistinguishably into each other.' Unreality, concealed absence, *das Unheimlich*, function here to reveal nothing. An 'it', not a 'he', Gregor as beetle circles slowly to a point of complete stasis, to be swept away as wastage with the refuse. Like *Frankenstein*, *Dracula*, and *Jekyll and Hyde*, *Metamorphosis* is structured around an Oedipal conflict. Father and son are set in opposition and the power of the first leaves no room for the second. The father's place (the bourgeois family home) is threatened by the space introduced by the son's metamorphosis (which effects a literal *emptying* of the domestic enclosure) and the father eradicates the threat by driving him to suicide. The son, Gregor, is compelled to become invisible, to cease to be, 'the decision that he must disappear was one that he held to'. He lapses into inarticulacy and blindness, 'day by day, things were growing dimmer to his sight', both of which draw attention to problems of *discourse* (he no longer uses his father's language) and of *vision* (he has lost the power of the look to control experience). Destroyed ('castrated') by the father, Gregor finds it impossible to move through the Oedipal stage and has 'to be got rid of'.

A semantic emptiness, present in Carroll, Lear, and much horror fiction, provides the centre of Kafka's work. Language slides away from things, as it does for Samsa, 'The words he uttered were no longer understandable'. Objects seem disconnected. 'Characters' fear they have no physical unity, they do not coincide with themselves. Structural confusion increases the circularity of quests for meaning, as impossible attempts are made to defeat semantic evasion. *The Great Wall of China* constructs fragments which will never add up to a whole meaning, for its human subjects do not understand 'the empire' which rules them. K., the anonymous non-identity at the centre of *The Trial* and *The Castle*, attempts to discover a significance which is known only by its absence. Like Godwin's *Caleb Williams*, *The Trial* delivers judgements which derive their sole authority from themselves: their 'law' is arbitrary yet unquestionable. *In the Penal Settlement* tells of a huge harrowing machine assuming a life of its own, tearing apart its officer when he offers himself as sacrifice. His horrific death has no meaning, 'no sign was visible of the promised redemption; what the others had found in the machine the officer had not found (. . .) through the forehead went the point of the great iron spike.' The subject of *The Hunger Artist* shrivels into a bundle of straw and is replaced by a panther. *Investigations of a Dog* is a canine journal, its narrator self *as* other. *The Burrow* is a fantasy of an underground creature, buried beneath 'a big hole, that leads nowhere', constructing endless subterranean passages. Its landscape is one of 'silence and emptiness'. Even rare epiphanies reveal nothing. Physical immolation, dismemberment, live burial, loss, death, metamorphosis, entropy, are no longer equivocal images, as they were in Gothic fiction. Kafka, in the wake of Dickens, Dostoevsky and Poe, makes them the norm, fantasies structured around the Oedipal drama.

His refusal of redemption has been called a 'negative transcendence', but this is to read Kafka as a mystic and to make his fantasies nostalgic. They are much less sentimental, more brutal. 'What is laid upon us', he writes, 'is to accomplish the negative, the positive is already given.' Maurice Blanchot (whose early fictions have similarities with Kafka's) has a phrase peculiarly appropriate to describe this fantastic effect: 'l'étrange roue ardente privée de centre' – a strange ardent wheel, deprived of a centre. The world is hollowed out by 'a nothing which demands to speak'. Kafka's closed mental spaces present nature's absences, omissions. Space is not freedom but is infinite imprisonment, as if the world were a prison with its bars meaninglessly open.

A literature with an excess of signifiers deprived of meaning finds an English equivalent to Kafka in the work of Mervyn Peake. Peake's elaborate construction of a Gothic enclosure of Gormenghast through his long, rambling, unfinished trilogy *Titus Groan, Gormenghast* and *Titus Alone* is close to Kafka's universe, without end(s). Peake's wandering hero, Titus, suffers the same deprivation of certainty as Kafka's K., never ceasing to look for an impossible, receding point of signification. Like Carroll's Alice, Peake's Titus is endlessly on the move, but arrives nowhere. Structurally, the trilogy defeats its own attempts to move forwards: a linear plot is frustrated by circular spirals backwards through lengthy descriptions of objects and material surroundings, rather like still film shots, holding up narrative action and flow. It produces a dynamic stasis, leading

nowhere. A convoluted baroque prose intensifies this effect of impossible movement, as if trapped by a restless energy which can only spend itself. Sentences are piled together, accumulated as units, any of which could be removed without the whole collapsing. Heaviness of the prose adds to the choking effect of Gormenghast, terribly material, dense, yet terribly vacuous, pregnant with emptiness: 'Gormenghast, that is, the main massing of the original stone, taken by itself would have displayed a certain ponderous architectural quality . . .' [3]

Lengthy, lush descriptions of the architecture amass material evidence to increase the sense of a claustrophobic, 'fallen' world:

> Because architecture is man-made and artificial, it [can] present states of mind with minute regard to texture and appearance as correlatives . . . It is also a supreme setting for 'Gothick' consciousness in that morbidity, decay, and desolation are unredeemed by any natural cyclic process. (Clifford, p.90)

Peake's fantasy (frequently using the term 'fantastic' to create its effects) is full of Dickensian grotesques, doubles, disembodied selves, and Gothic motifs. Initially, his grotesques simply 'are', present as the half-living matter which makes up the world of Gormenghast. Only gradually does his tale move forwards from stasis to be drawn into a plot where figures function as romance agents in a magical narrative of good (Titus) against evil (Steerpike). This romance element has aligned Peake with Tolkien as a modern fabulist, but there are few similarities. Peake refuses nostalgia. He offers no false promise of redemption. 'The walls of Gormenghast were like the walls of paradise or the walls of an inferno. The colours were devilish or angelical according to the colour of the mind that watched them.' His Gormenghast books can be read as partial allegories of the horrors of World War II, with Steerpike roughly corresponding to Hitler and a defeat of 'evil' as a victory against Nazism.

Unlike *The Lord of the Rings*, though, moral victory is not assumed as a foregone conclusion. 'Nature' is not in itself redemptive. Titus 'ends' where he began, in a hell of microcosm, on an endless quest for meaning:

> From time to time, as they sped through the upper atmosphere, and while the world unveiled itself . . . it seemed that the earth wandered through his skull . . . a cosmos in the bone; a universe lit by a hundred lights and thronged by shapes and shadows; alive with endless threads of circumstance . . . action and event. All futility: disordered; with no end and no beginning. (*Titus Alone*, p.258)

Literature as manifestly unreal, as fabrication, as lie: this is another branch of the modern fantastic. It is evident in the wonderful linguistic fantasies of Jorge Louis Borges, in his *Extraordinary Tales, Labyrinths, Fictions* and *Book of Imaginary Beings*. Borges describes 'the polished surfaces' of his books as able to 'represent and promise the infinite'. His fantasy worlds of Tlön, Uqbar and Orbis Tertius exist as signs referring only to themselves, self-generated.[4] Novels by Barthelme, Coover, Hawkes, Malamud, Vonnegut, have been related to this tradition of fantasy as fabulation, as metafiction. John Barth's *Giles Goat Boy, Chimera, The Sot Weed Factor, Lost in the Funhouse*, play with literary fantasies as interchangeable, autonomous texts. Robert Scholes discusses all these works as self-reflexive, playing upon their own fictionality.[5]

Their non-referentiality, though, makes them different in function from pure fantasies, which have been seen to be defined by their problematical relation to and representation of the 'real'. Novels by Dostoevsky, Dickens, Kafka, and a literature of the double, set up an internal dialogue between 'real' and 'unreal', 'self' and 'other', whereas modern metafictions are set apart, taking pleasure in their manifest unreality by presenting only a series of reversible representations. From Breton's *Nadja* to Dylan's

*Tarantula* (1971), surrealistic fantasies are also set apart, imitating a dream world or a fractured external world, but not breaking structures of the real *within* the text: neither metafictions nor purely surrealistic fictions break the axis of the real: for them it is already broken.

More dialogical in structure are Italo Calvino's self-conscious fantasies, *Cosmicomics*, *t zero*, *The Nonexistent Knight*, *The Castle of Crossed Destinies* and *Invisible Cities*. These construct 'other' worlds, within which relations of real-unreal are constantly interrogated. *Invisible Cities* (1972) is made up of a dialogue between Marco Polo and Kublai Khan, talking about impossible places which exist within, or around, real ones. A real city, Venice, is mentioned, but it is present only as a negative version of itself. There is no absolute 'city' which can be known. Any place is capable of metamorphosing into its own other.

> Differences are lost: each city takes to resembling all cities, places exchange their form, order, distances, a shapeless dust cloud invades the continents. The catalogue of forms is endless: until every shape has found its city, new cities will continue to be born.[6]

A latent otherness is constantly exerting pressure to be released in Calvino's fiction. 'All the future Berenices are already present in this instant, wrapped one within the other, confined, crammed, inextricable' (p.125). Marco Polo tells Kublai Khan that 'Your footsteps follow not what is outside the eyes, but what is within, buried, erased' (p.73). Calvino's world is always unfamiliar.

Fantasy, then, has not disappeared, as Todorov's theory would claim, but it has assumed different forms. With Kafka and Calvino, 'truth' remains an evasive, impossible object, as it had been for Mary Shelley, Maturin and Hogg. Their fantasies are equally hollowed out by a consciousness of 'the sacred' as something absent.

Thomas Pynchon's fantasies are, in many ways, a consummation of that kind of 'fantastic realism' found in Dickens, Dostoevsky and Kafka. Pynchon's tales *Mortality and Mercy in Vienna* (1959), *Lowlands* (1960), *Entropy* (1960) and his novels, *V* (1963), *The Crying of Lot 49* (1966), *Gravity's Rainbow* (1973), are built upon a structure which is *oxymoronic*, an establishment of mutually contradictory statement and impossibility. *Mortality and Mercy in Vienna* makes mercy and death equivalent in an impossible equation. *Entropy* makes explicit that pull towards a condition of undifferentiation which we have seen to be a central feature of literary fantasy, but it identifies it as a cultural phenomenon, not as something located solely in the individual. Pynchon's prose itself gathers together a massive amount of cultural material as if it were so much waste matter, the waste of 'culture', culture *as* waste, or garbage or excrement, expressed on the page. What Bakhtin detected as a determining force in Dostoevsky's polyphonic texts – a mixture of discrete elements, a promiscuity characteristic of the collapse of all divisions in modern society (except for the divide between labour and capital) – is the ruling principle in Pynchon's fiction.

*Entropy*, set in Washington in 1957, takes the idea of entropy as its central metaphor and as its narrative method, as everything collides together. The hermetically sealed world of Callisto and Aubade, two romantics in a hot-house in the upper storey of a block of flats, is unable to resist disintegration. External disorder and chaos – represented by the noisy, messy world below, in the apartment of Meatball Mulligan – spreads out to absorb their form and difference. Opposed to their classical music is the improvised jazz from below, and Aubade's serenity is disturbed by 'hints of anarchy: gaps and excrescences and skew lines' rising from below. The whole tale is pulled towards its final, entropic darkness. Entropy, 'the measure of disorganization for a closed system', becomes applicable to the world itself, the half-living world of American consumerism. Callisto detects in this secularized culture 'a similar tendency' (as in any organism) to progress 'from the least to the most probable, from differentiation to sameness, from ordered individuality to a kind of chaos.' [7]

Callisto is obsessed with the concept of entropy. (His favourite authors are Sade, Faulkner, Djuna Barnes and Henry Miller, with their sense of 'correspondences'.) The second law of thermodynamics embodies the principle: it holds that the energy of any system is insufficient to prevent it from running down. Any system will eventually decline, 'galaxy, engine, human being, culture, whatever' will gradually sink to 'the condition of the More Probable', to a zero point of non-difference. Pynchon provides a scientific rationalization of the entropic movement found in fantastic literature, and thereby points to the impossibility of effective resistance, for all struggle is finally resolved in that undifferentiation, that 'tonic of darkness and the final absence of all motion'. Entropy does not function metaphorically for Pynchon, but literally: it is apprehended as the condition of life, and one which is peculiarly appropriate as an expression of the world running down with consumer culture. He tells of the exhaustion of sacred and of secular systems alike.

The lengthy trajectories of *V* and of *Gravity's Rainbow* accumulate cultural 'waste' in their kaleidoscoping of a mass of heterogeneous cultural references, from literature, film, music, history, science. Religious myths are betrayed as being anachronistic and secular ones as being tawdry. There are few signs of whole 'character' here, for people and objects merge together, become one mass of waste matter. Like Alfred Jarry's Faustian subject in *Dr Faustroll*, who is secreted away as the excrement of culture (reminiscent of Kafka's buried narrators), Pynchon's Fausto in *V* is part of the world's rubble, sharing 'much of the non-humanity of the debris, crushed stone, broken masonry, destroyed churches and auberges of his city'. As in Dickens, the material world in Pynchon has taken control, and the 'human', the controlling 'I', has ceased to be effective in imposing order as difference or significance. *Gravity's Rainbow* (which one critic terms 'the metaphysical opposite of God's grace', cit. Siegel, p.73) represents a vast undifferentiated 'reality'. In 'this transmarginal leap, this surrender . . . ideas of the opposite have come together, and lost their oppositeness'. ' "I'm no longer sure which of all the words, images, dreams or ghosts are 'yours' and which are 'mine'. It's past sorting out. We're both being someone new now, someone incredible".' [8]

Pynchon presents strange mixtures of too much and of nothing as the condition of Western consumerism: an excess of matter, an excess of cultural signs deprived of absolute meaning. He parodies apocalyptic visions, refusing transcendent solutions, despite the quest for final answers, for a key that will 'bring us back' lying lost somewhere 'among the wastes of the world' (*Gravity's Rainbow*). The dense narrative of *The Crying of Lot 49* links the impossibility of such a quest to its situation within the symbolic. Here, the protagonist, Oedipa Maas (her name immediately associates her with Oedipus and the problem of the Oedipal stage in entering culture), is faced with the impossibility of deciphering the system (the signifying practice) of the culture in which she is placed. She is engaged with an attempt to resist 'a pull towards disorder, to re-sort events into a stelliferous meaning'. By explicit references to the great 'Other', Pynchon draws attention to the relation of this tale to Lacanian theory and the difficult situation of the subject in tension between the imaginary and the symbolic.

Like many predecessors in literary fantasies from Godwin's *Caleb Williams* to Kafka's *Metamorphosis*, Pynchon's Oedipa is unable to arrive at any definitive understanding of the nature of the 'real'. Even more dramatically than in previous works, the subject here is subject to something called 'paranoia' – delusions of persecution – yet here the paranoia cannot be placed in the self: it is embedded in the world around her and she is unable to arrive at the 'truth' of its origins. What Oedipa apprehends as 'Otherness' is written into the world at large, as 'something blind, soulless; a brute automatism that led to external death ... a brute Other', heard in 'disembodied voices from whose malignance there was no appeal', seen in 'the soft dusk of mirrors out of which something was about to walk, encountered in empty rooms that waited for her'.[9] 'Possibilities for paranoia become abundant.'

Oedipa is left a fortune, and in her hunting down of its origins discovers a vast network of signs and symbols constituting a secret system of correspondences, a system of WASTE. This secret network of hostile forces determining individual lives operates against the construction of independent, viable 'selves'. Confronted with such a symbolic system, Oedipa experiences herself as disintegrating, as ex-centric, unreal. The complex refracted narrative filters events through Oedipa's unseeing perspective so that the reader too is confused and disordered, unable to situate him or herself clearly in relation to what is apprehended 'out there'. Equivocation is no longer confined to an individual, misapprehending subject, but has spread to suggest the impossibility of establishing anything 'real' independent of that contradictory system of signification. Oedipa longs for the whole thing to *be* mere fantasy: 'She wanted it all to be a fantasy – some clear result of her several wounds, needs, dark doubles', for 'the chance of its being real' is infinitely disturbing.

Yet the narrative provides no definitive resolution. It leaves the subject, Oedipa, in the space between the imaginary and the symbolic, unable to return to the unities of the first and unable to understand the 'meaning' of the second. The ending is a suspending, an irresolution. 'Oedipa settled back, to await the crying of lot 49', in which the 'key', the code, might be provided. Such a rapid account as this of Pynchon's narrative hardly engages with its complexities, and it needs extensive relation to Lacan's theoretical model. But Pynchon's work can be read as fantastic narrative which is fully self-conscious of its implications. A system of paranoia seems to have an objective correlative in his tales of subjects tormented by a vast, persecuting network – the WASTE system of consumer culture itself.

A fantastic mode, structured upon contradiction, upon an 'impossibility', becomes a disturbingly appropriate medium in Pynchon's texts to represent the fullness and emptiness of secularized culture. Oedipa oscillates between signs and meanings, wondering if there is an absolute signified which might introduce sense into her world:

> It was now like walking among matrices of a great digital computer, the zeroes and ones twinned above, hanging like balanced mobiles right and left, ahead, thick, maybe endless. Behind the hieroglyphic streets there would either be a transcendent meaning, or only the earth . . . Another mode of meaning behind the obvious, or none. (pp.136–7)

Pynchon's fantasies leave the question unresolved, posing the quest for signification amidst a chaos of signs, as their central concern. Their apprehension of hollowness, of absence, of emptiness coincides with a radical questioning of contemporary culture, and its elevation of matter and of materialism over all other values. For 'never in any previous civilization have the great metaphysical preoccupations, the fundamental questions of being and of the meaning of life, seemed so utterly remote and pointless' (Jameson, *Marxism and Form*, p.xviii).

# 8 AFTERWORD: THE 'UNSEEN' OF CULTURE

I look elsewhere and differently, there where there is no spectacle.

Hélène Cixous[1]

The crucial thing is not what is behind the images, but what is visible in them as a speck of white. The beyond . . . is the repressed, censored portion of the 'this-side' of things . . . the raising of the dead, that is in fact the real triumph of disorder. An event beyond all interpretability, outside any context. A zero point, another white speck, a gap in the chain of causality. When Freud began to describe the Unconscious and to comprehend it in a theoretical manner he could only establish that he was in an area where the conceptual apparatus of the existing sciences broke down. That it was the great Other on which we all depend, and which, at first, could only be conceptualized by means of negative categories.

Frieda Grafe[2]

THROUGHOUT its 'history', fantasy has been obscured and locked away, buried as something inadmissible and darkly shameful. Spenser's long allegorical poem, *The Faerie Queene*, locks away the giant

Phantastes, spinner of endless fantasies, in a dark chamber concealed within the centre of the House of Temperance. Phantastes is significantly hidden within the mansion of order and propriety, left to spin

> Infinite shapes of thinges dispersed thin;
> Some such as in the world were never yit,
> Ne can devized be of mortall wit.[3]

The fantastic has constantly been dismissed by critics as being an embrace of madness, irrationality, or barbarism and it has been opposed to the humane and more civilized practices of 'realistic' literature. Belinsky, for example, condemned Dostoevsky's *The Double* for its 'fantastic colouring', declaring that 'The fantastic in our time can have a place only in an insane asylum, and not in our literature' (Belinsky, cit. Wasiolek, p.5). Walter Scott similarly dismissed E.T.A. Hoffmann's tales for hovering on the edge of insanity and for not being 'reconciled to taste'.

An implicit association of the fantastic with the barbaric and non-human has exiled it to the edges of literary culture. Novelists redeploying some fantastic elements, such as Dickens, Gogol, or Dostoevsky, have been placed differently from Jane Austen, George Eliot, or Henry James, in the establishment of a canon of 'great' literature, whilst Gothic novelists, Sade, M.G. Lewis, Mary Shelley, James Hogg, R.L. Stevenson, Calvino, have been relatively neglected. Only recently has the influence of French theory begun to encourage a less hostile reading of and response to these fantastic texts and begun to formulate some of the critical problems which they articulate – problems which need much more extensive discussion than has been possible in this book, problems to do with the relation between language and *eros*, to do with the 'unconscious' formation of the subject, the interplay of imaginary, symbolic and real, and the violent intersection of 'fantastic' narratives in the midst of this interplay. Precisely because it is situated in this crucial area, the fantastic demands much more theoretical attention, in relation to literary and film texts, and much more analysis of its linguistic and psychoanalytical features.

Not surprisingly, fantastic art has been muted by a tradition of literary criticism concerned with supporting establishment ideals rather than with subverting them. In so far as it is possible to reconstruct a 'history' of literary fantasy, it is one of repeated neutralization of its images of impossibility and of desire – both in the trajectories of the literary texts themselves and in the criticism which has mediated them to an intellectual audience.

The dismissal of the fantastic to the margins of literary culture is in itself an ideologically significant gesture, one which is not dissimilar to culture's silencing of unreason. As an 'art' of unreason, and of desire, fantasy has persistently been silenced, or re-written, in transcendental rather than transgressive terms. Its threatened un-doing, or dissolution, of dominant structures, has been re-made, re-covered into moral allegory and magical romance. As Foucault writes of unreason, 'Any transgression in life becomes a social crime, condemned and punished . . . imprisoned in a moral world [for offending] bourgeois society.' [4] From a rational, 'monological' world, otherness cannot be known or represented except as foreign, irrational, 'mad', 'bad'. It is either rejected altogether, or polemically refuted, or assimilated into a 'meaningful' narrative structure, re-written or written out as romance or as fable. Otherness is transmuted into idealism by romance writers and is muted, made silent and invisible by 'realistic' works, only to return in strange, expressive forms in many texts. The 'other' expressed through fantasy has been categorized as a negative black area – as evil, demonic, barbaric – until its recognition in the modern fantastic as culture's 'unseen'.

Fantasies moving towards the realm of the 'marvellous' are the ones which have been tolerated and widely disseminated socially. A creation of secondary worlds through religious myth, faery, science fiction, uses 'legalized' methods – religion, magic, science – to establish other worlds, worlds which are *compensatory*, which fill up a lack, making up for an apprehension of actuality as disordered and insufficient. These fantasies *transcend* that actuality. Their romance base suggests that the universe is, ultimately, a self-regulating mechanism in which goodness, stability, order will eventually prevail. They serve to stabilize social order by minimizing the need for human intervention in this benevolently organized cosmic mechanism.

Critics of fantasy have tended to defend it in terms of this *transcendent* function. One of the first apologists was Charles Nodier, whose essay 'The fantastic in literature' was published by the *Revue de Paris* in 1830. Nodier detected a line of continuity between religious and secular fantasies: the second were a later development of the first and had a similar cultural function, to tell tales of escaping, or of transcending, the human condition.[5] As late as 1973, Jean-Baptiste Baronian echoes this sentiment in an article defining 'the property of the fantastic' as being 'to transcend reality, even beyond the most elementary sounds and voices' (Baronian, p.14). French critics such as Caillois, Lévy and Vax, English critics including John Batchelor, C.N. Manlove and Stephen Prickett, have all passed on this notion of the fantastic as an escapist literature and have made this the centre of their apologies. The works of the last three are situated within an academic tradition of liberal humanist criticism, to which transcendentalism is no stranger, but it leaves their ideas cut off from those vital theoretical areas essential to an understanding of the fantastic.

In many ways these traditional defendants of fantasy are repeating one of Freud's ideas as to the cultural function of art itself. The creation of artistic products, according to Freud, is a 'phantasizing' activity which provides man with compensation for having renounced instinctive gratification. 'Men have always found it hard to renounce pleasure', writes Freud. 'They cannot bring themselves to do it without some kind of compensation' (*Introductory Lectures on Psychoanalysis*, p.419). When fantasy has been allowed to surface within culture, it has been in a manner close to Freud's notion of art as compensation, as an activity which *sustains* cultural order by making up for a society's lacks. Gothic fiction, for example, tended to buttress a dominant, bourgeois, ideology, by vicarious wish fulfilment through fantasies of incest, rape, murder, parricide, social disorder. Like pornography, it functioned to supply an object of desire, to imagine social and sexual transgression.

Merely on a thematic level, then, fantastic literature is not necessarily subversive. To attempt to defend fantasy as inherently transgressive would be a vast, over-simplifying and mistaken gesture. Those elements which have been designated 'fantastic' – effecting a movement towards undifferentiation and a condition of entropy – have been constantly re-worked, re-written and re-covered to *serve* rather than to *subvert* the dominant ideology. As Jonathan Culler writes, 'For the most part, fantasy in literature testifies to the power of the reality principle to transform its enemies into its own mirror image. In the face of this power, it is all the more important that we assert fantasy's responsibility to resist before we accept Yeats's formula: "In dreams begins responsibility" ' (Culler, 'Literary Fantasy', p.33).

An understanding of the subversive function of fantastic literature emerges from *structuralist* rather than from merely *thematic* readings of texts. It has been seen that many fantasies from the late eighteenth century onwards attempt to undermine dominant philosophical and epistemological orders. They subvert and interrogate nominal unities of time, space and character, as well as questioning the possibility, or honesty, of fictional re-presentation of those unities. Like the grotesque,[6] with which it overlaps, the fantastic can be seen as an art of estrangement, resisting closure, opening structures which categorize experience in the name of a 'human reality'. By drawing attention to the relative nature of these categories the fantastic moves towards a dismantling of the 'real', most particularly of the concept of 'character' and its ideological assumptions, mocking and parodying a blind faith in psychological coherence and in the value of sublimation as a 'civilizing' activity.

A unified, stable 'ego' lies at the heart of this systematic coherence and the fantastic explodes this by seeking to make that heart's darkness visible. From Hoffmann and German Romanticism, to the modern fantastic in horror films, fantasy has tried to erode the pillars of society by un-doing categorical structures. As Hélène Cixous writes, 'The machine of repression has always had the same accomplices; homogenizing, reductive, unifying reason has always allied itself to the Master, to the single, stable, socializable subject, represented by its types or characters.' In fantastic works where the 'I' is more than one, there is a resistance to such reduction. 'These texts baffle every attempt to summarization of meaning and limiting, repressive interpretation. The subject flounders here in the exploded multiplicity of its states ... spreading out in every possible direction ... transegoistically.' They erode the supports of 'logocentism, idealism, theologism, the scaffolding of political and subjective economy' ('The character of "character" ', p.389). ·

Far from construing this attempt at erosion as a mere embrace of barbarism or of chaos, it is possible to discern it as a desire for something excluded from cultural order – more specifically, for all that is in opposition to the capitalist and patriarchal order which has been dominant in Western society over the last two centuries. As a literature of desire, the fantastic can be seen as providing a point of departure, in Bersani's words, 'for an authentically civilizing scepticism about the nature of our desires and the nature of our being' (p.313).

Irène Bessière's study of fantasy indicated its position as one of *relationality*, as a narrative situated in a relation of opposition to dominant orders. Bessière connects this function to Sartre's distinction between the *non-thetic* as opposed to the *thetic* (c.f. p.75). The fantastic, in its movement

towards non-signification, pulls towards the non-thetic, to all that is opposed to dominant signifying practice. The theoretical work of Julia Kristeva suggests that the non-thetic can be linked to all those forces which threaten to disrupt a tradition of rationalism. Such forces have been apprehended as inimical to cultural order from at least as far back as Plato's *Republic*. Plato expelled from his ideal Republic all transgressive energies, all those energies which have been seen to be expressed through the fantastic: eroticism, violence, madness, laughter, nightmares, dreams, blasphemy, lamentation, uncertainty, female energy, excess. Art which represented such energies was to be exiled from Plato's ideal state. Literature mentioning 'the Rivers of Wailing and Gloom, and the ghosts of corpses, and all other things whose very names are enough to make everyone who hears them shudder' was to have *no place* in the Republic. The working life of slaves, the oppression of women, or any intimation of their suffering, any reference to sexuality or childbirth, were similarly banned from fictional representation. Socrates and his audience agree that 'We must forbid this sort of thing entirely' (*The Republic*, pp.141–2). The fantastic, then, is *made invisible* in Plato's Republic and in the tradition of high rationalism which it fostered: alongside all subversive social forces, fantasy is expelled and is registered only as absence. 'Plato feels his rational and unified Republic threatened from within by forces, desires and activities which must be censored or ostracized if the rational state is to be maintained' (White, p.3).

Through the introduction of some of the theories of Freud and of Lacan, it has been possible to claim for the fantastic a subversive function in attempting to depict a *reversal* of the subject's cultural formation. If the symbolic is seen as 'that unity of semantic and syntactic competence which allows communication and rationality to appear' (White, p.8), the imaginary area which is intimated in fantastic literature suggests all that is other, all that is absent from the symbolic, outside rational discourse. Fantasies of deconstructed, demolished or divided identities and of dis-integrated bodies, oppose traditional categories of unitary selves. They attempt to give graphic depictions of subjects *in process*, suggesting possibilities of innumerable other selves, of different histories, different bodies. They denounce the theses and categories of the thetic, attempting to dissolve the symbolic order at its very base, where it is established in and through the subject, where the dominant signifying system is re-produced. This does not imply that subjects can exist outside of ideology and of the social formation, but that fantasies image the possibility of radical cultural transfor-mation through attempting to dissolve or shatter the boun-dary lines between the imaginary and the symbolic. They refuse the latter's categories of the 'real' and its unities.

The modern fantastic, as exemplified for instance in the tales of Kafka, does not simply embrace chaos, nor does a theoretical approach to these texts simply urge a lapse into the pre-linguistic or pre-cultural. As Kafka's *Metamorphosis* makes clear, it is not a matter of seeking a dissolution of 'civilizing' forms as such, nor of advocating a 'new bar-barism'. Rather it is a matter of apprehending the symbolic as repressive and crippling to the subject, and of attempting to transform the relations between the symbolic and the imaginary. Kafka's Gregor Samsa has no simple desire for death: the tale incorporates as part of its internal structure a tension between the symbolic and the imaginary, expressing a reluctance to give in to a desire for something other, yet apprehending this other as the only alternative to a hostile, patriarchal order. Kafka is well aware of the de-humanizing implications of fantastic transformation, and the dilemma articulated here is central to modern fantasy.

> But what if all the quiet, the comfort, the contentment were now to end in horror? ... Did he really want his warm room, so comfortably fitted with old family fur-niture, to be turned into a naked den in which he would certainly be able to crawl unhampered in all directions

but at the price of shedding simultaneously all recollection of his human background?[7]

To introduce the fantastic is to replace familiarity, comfort, *das Heimlich*, with estrangement, unease, the uncanny. It is to introduce dark areas, of something completely other and unseen, the spaces outside the limiting frame of the 'human' and 'real', outside the control of the 'word' and of the 'look'. Hence the association of the modern fantastic with the horrific, from Gothic tales of terror to contemporary horror films. The emergence of such literature in periods of relative 'stability' (the mid-eighteenth century, late nineteenth century, mid-twentieth century) points to a direct relation between cultural repression and its generation of oppositional energies which are *expressed* through various forms of fantasy in art.

Fantasy has always articulated a longing for imaginary unity, for unity in the realm of the imaginary. In this sense, it is inherently idealistic. It expresses a desire for an absolute, for an absolute signified, an absolute meaning. It is no accident that the Faust motif is so central, recurring explicitly or implicitly in post-Romantic fantasies and fictions from *Vathek, Frankenstein, Melmoth the Wanderer* and *Confessions of a Justified Sinner*, through Balzac's *Louis Lambert* and *La recherche de L'absolu*, to Alfred Jarry's *Dr Faustroll*, Mann's *Doctor Faustus* and Pynchon's *V*, for Faust signifies precisely this desire, within a secularized culture. Whereas fantasies produced from within a religious or magical thought mode depict the possibility of union of self and other, fantasies without those systems of belief cannot realize absolute 'truth' or 'unity'. Their longings for otherness are apprehended as impossible, except in parodic, travestied, horrific or tragic form.

Like its mythical and magical predecessors, then, the fantastic desires transformation and difference. Unlike its transcendental counterparts (found in recent 'faery' literature), the fantastic refuses to accept supernatural fictions: it remains non-nostalgic, without illusions of superhuman intervention to effect difference. 'The great realizations of the modern fantastic – the last unrecognizable avatars of romance as a mode – draw their magical power from their *unsentimental* loyalty to those henceforth abandoned clearings across which higher and lower worlds once passed' (Jameson, p.146, my italics). As Todorov pointed out, fantasy is located uneasily between 'reality' and 'literature', unable to accept either, with the result that a fantastic mode is situated between the 'realistic' and the 'marvellous', stranded between this world and the next. Its subversive function derives from this uneasy positioning. The negative versions (inversions) of unity, found in the modern fantastic, from Gothic novels – Mary Shelley, Elizabeth Gaskell, Dickens, Poe, Dostoevsky, Stevenson, Wilde – to Kafka, Cortázar, Calvino, Lovecraft, Peake and Pynchon, represent dissatisfaction and frustration with a cultural order which deflects or defeats desire, yet refuse to have recourse to compensatory, transcendental otherworlds.

The modern fantastic, the form of literary fantasy within the secularized culture produced by capitalism, is a subversive literature. It exists alongside the 'real', on either side of the dominant cultural axis, as a muted presence, a silenced imaginary other. Structurally and semantically, the fantastic aims at dissolution of an order experienced as oppressive and insufficient. Its paraxial placing, eroding and scrutinizing the 'real', constitutes, in Hélène Cixous's phrase, 'a subtle invitation to transgression'. By attempting to transform the relations between the imaginary and the symbolic, fantasy hollows out the 'real', revealing its absence, its 'great Other', its unspoken and its unseen. As Todorov writes, 'The fantastic permits us to cross certain frontiers that are inaccessible so long as we have no recourse to it'.

# NOTES

## 1 Introduction

1 Franz Kafka, *Metamorphosis and Other Stories*, tr. by Willa and Edwin Muir (London, 1961), pp.71–3.
2 Juliet Mitchell, *Psychoanalysis and Feminism*, p.xvi.
3 Fredric Jameson, 'Magical narratives: romance as genre'.
4 Sigmund Freud, *Introductory Lectures on Psychoanalysis*, pp.206–7.
5 Sigmund Freud, *The Psychopathology of Everyday Life*, cit. Todorov, p.161.

## 2 The fantastic as a mode

1 Julia Kristeva, 'Une poétique ruinée', p.15: 'The "fantastic", the "oneiric", the "sexual" speak of this same *dialogism*, this unfinished polyphony, which is unsayable.'
2 Louia Vax, 'L'art de faire peur', p.929.
3 To refer to an 'economy' of ideas and beliefs might seem strange: by 'natural economy' a system of secularized thought is meant as opposed to a 'supernatural' order.

The relation of 'economies' to cultural beliefs in this metaphorical sense has been explored by Bataille, with his notion of *potlach*, or 'waste' – that which is in excess of what is needed. See Gillman's thesis.

4  Guy de Maupassant, *Horla*, in *Selected Short Stories*, tr. by Roger Colet (London, 1971), pp.330–1.

5  Gogol, *The Nose*, in *Diary of a Madman and Other Stories*, tr. by Ronald Wilks (London, 1972), p.70.

6  Brothers Grimm, *The Complete Grimm's Fairy Tales* (London, 1975), p.497.

7  Charles Kingsley, *Water Babies* (London, 1863), p.1.

8  Edgar Allan Poe, *Selected Writings* (London, 1967).

9  For discussion of the relation of mimetic forms of the novel to bourgeois ideology, see works by Belsey, Eagleton, Jameson, Knight and Watt in the bibliography.

10  J.H. Matthews (ed.), *The Custom-House of Desire: A Half-Century of Surrealist Stories* (London, 1975), p.239.

11  H.P. Lovecraft, *At the Mountains of Madness and Other Novels of Terror* (London, 1968).

12  H.P. Lovecraft, *The Tomb and Other Tales* (London, 1969), p.176.

13  ibid., p.184.

14  Cit. Cora Kaplan, 'Language and gender', p.36.

15  W.H. Auden's *Secondary Worlds* influenced Tolkien's formulation of secondary, autonomous, imagined realms in *Tree and Leaf*. These regions are close to those described by C.S. Lewis in *Of Other Worlds*, where he identifies as a primal desire of man an 'imaginative impulse . . . working under the special conditions of our time . . . to visit strange regions in search of such beauty, awe or terror as the actual world does not supply'. The transcendentalism of Auden, Tolkien and Lewis is analogous to the 'marvellous' regions of fairy tale and traditional romance, and is in marked contrast to the more transgressive thrust of the modern fantastic in secular writings, which present the strangeness and otherness of *this* world.

16 *The Complete Works of Lewis Carroll*, p.134.
17 George MacDonald, *Phantastes and Lilith* (London, 1962), p.224.
18 ibid., p.202.
19 H.G. Wells, *Selected Short Stories* (London, 1958), pp. 106–22.
20 Valery Brussof, *The Mirror*, in *The Republic of the Southern Cross and Other Stories* (London, 1918), pp.55–72.
21 R.L. Stevenson, *The Strange Case of Dr Jekyll and Mr Hyde* (London, 1925), p.51.
22 Italo Calvino, *Invisible Cities*, tr. by William Weaver (London, 1979), p.26.
23 William Morris, *The Hollow Land*, in *Early Romances in Prose and Verse* (London, 1973), p.261.
24 H.P. Lovecraft, *The Book*, in *The Tomb and Other Tales*, pp. 184–5.
25 Mary Shelley, *Collected Tales and Stories*, ed. Charles E. Robinson (London, 1976).
26 Gérard de Nerval, *Aurélia*, cit. Todorov, p.119.
27 Bram Stoker, *Dracula* (New York, 1965), pp. 9, 10.
28 Fyodor Dostoevsky, *The Brothers Karamazov*, tr. by David Magarshack, 2 vols. (London, 1958), p.749.

## 3  Psychoanalytical perspectives

1 Adalbert von Chamisso, *Peter Schlemihl*, tr. by Leopold von Lowenstein-Wertheim (London, 1957), p.20.
2 Bulwer Lytton, *Zanoni: A Rosicrucian Tale* (New York, 1971).
3 *The Complete Works of Lewis Carroll*, p.382.
4 *Dracula*, p.19 and p.88.
5 'The Uncanny', *Standard Edition of the Complete Psychological Works of Sigmund Freud*, vol. 17, pp.217–52.
6 E.T.A. Hoffmann, *The Sandman*, in *The Best Tales of Hoffmann*, ed. E.F. Bleiler (New York, 1967), pp. 183–214.
7 See, for example, works by Bonaparte, Brooke-Rose,

Robert in the bibliography.

8 Gillian Beer, 'Ghosts', a review article of Julia Briggs's survey of English ghost fiction, *Night Visitors*, p.260.

9 Sade, *Justine, Philosophy in the Bedroom, Eugénie de Franval and Other Writings*, tr. by Richard Seaver and Austryn Wainhouse (New York, 1965), pp.186–7.

10 Sade, cit. Klossowski in his essay 'Nature as destructive principle', reprinted in *The 120 Days of Sodom* (New York, 1966), pp.65–86 (p.71).

11 Sade, 'Dialogue between a priest and a dying man', from *Justine*, p.173.

12 Hubert Damisch, 'L'écriture sans mesures', from *Tel Quel* 28 (Winter, 1967), an issue devoted to 'La pensée de Sade', which includes other important articles on the problematics of language and desire, e.g. Philippe Sollers, 'Sade dans le texte' and Roland Barthes, 'L'arbre du crime'. See works by Barthes and Klossowski in the bibliography.

13 Sade, *Justine*, p.169.

14 Comte de Lautréamont, *Maldoror and Poems*, tr. by Paul Knight (London, 1978), p.170.

15 Ann Quin, *Berg* (London, 1977), pp.22–3.

16 Freud, *Beyond the Pleasure Principle*, p.56.

17 Poe, *Selected Writings*, p.131.

18 Poe, *Science Fiction* (London, 1976), pp.96–7.

19 Ovid, *Metamorphoses*, tr. by Mary M. Innes (London, 1955), p.43.

20 Rimbaud, *Collected Poems* (London, 1962), p.6.

21 See Bersani on the theatre of Artaud and Chaikin.

22 Roald Dahl, *Tales of the Unexpected* (London, 1979), p.175.

23 Gérard de Nerval, 'Aurélia', *Oeuvres* (Paris, 1966), pp.782–3.

24 *The Complete Works of Lewis Carroll*, p.464.

25 MacDonald, *Phantastes and Lilith* (London, 1962), p.195.

26 Controversy over Lacan's theories and their usefulness for materialist criticism is ongoing. I have not attemp-

ted to engage with current arguments in this book, merely to suggest that literary fantasies can be approached as expressions of those elements in the subject's psychic life which do not conform to the demands of his or her social positioning. See Weedon's study in the bibliography.

27  Recent criticism tends to employ these two terms in a way derived from Lacan and Kristeva, but more generally. The 'symbolic order' designates 'the apparent unity of the dominant ideological discourses in play at any one time' (Hebdige, p.119).

28  *La révolution du langage poétique*. The most lucid introduction to Kristeva's theories is to be found in Allon White's article, 'L'éclatement du sujet'.

## 4  Gothic tales and novels

1  See Foucault, *The Order of Things* and Gay Clifford, *The Transformations of Allegory* for philosophical and literary discussions of this change.

2  Hawkes, *Structuralism and Semiotics*, p.146, refers to Derrida's *L'écriture et la différence* for a study of the effects of a loss of a 'transcendental signified' on man's use of signs and their meanings.

3  Railo, Varma, Summers, Tompkins, Lévy, Karl and Kiely are listed in the bibliography.

4  William Godwin, *The Adventures of Caleb Williams, or Things as They Are* (London, 1966).

5  Mary W. Shelley, *Frankenstein, or the Modern Prometheus*, ed. M.K. Joseph (London, 1969); *The Last Man*, ed. Hugh J. Luke, Jr. (Nebraska, 1965).

6  For film versions, see the section 'The visual progeny: drama and film' in Levine and Knoepflmacher's *The Endurance of Frankenstein*, and René Prédal's *Le cinéma fantastique*.

7  Cit. Todorov, p.117.

8  Volney, *Ruins of Empires* (London, undated), p.4.

9 This anticipates Artaud's metaphorical use of the plague in *The Theatre and its Double*: 'Society's barriers became fluid with the effects of the scourge. Order disappeared. He witnessed the subversion of all morality, the breakdown of all psychology.' (p.7).

10 Ellen Moers, *Literary Women*, pp.90–110, identifies a tradition of 'female Gothic'. It is surely no coincidence that so many writers and theorists of fantasy as a countercultural form are women – Julia Kristeva, Irène Bessière, Hélène Cixous, Angela Carter. Non-realist narrative forms are increasingly important in feminist writing: no breakthrough of cultural structure seems possible until linear narrative (realism, illusionism, transparent representation) is broken or dissolved.

11 C.R. Maturin, *Melmoth the Wanderer* (Oxford, 1968), p.236.

12 Gifford's *James Hogg*, pp.141–2, records Hogg's debt to Walpole, Radcliffe, Godwin, Lewis, Hoffmann, Mary Shelley, and Maturin.

13 Anonymous review, *Westminster Review*, October 1824, pp.560–2.

14 William Blake, 'Notes on the illustrations to Dante', *Complete Writings* (Oxford, 1966), p.785.

15 Friedrich Schlegel, *The Philosophy of Life and the Philosophy of Language* (London, 1847), p.389.

16 G.W.F. Hegel, *The Phenomenology of Mind* (1807), tr. by J.B. Baillie, pp.77–8.

17 Poe, *Selected Stories*, p.264. This horror of absence is repeated in H.G. Wells's fantasy, *The Invisible Man*, whose protagonist is mere space: 'a vast and incredible mouth that swallowed up the whole of the lower portion of his face ... It was so uncanny.' *The Invisible Man* (London, 1959), pp. 29, 32.

18 Poe, *Selected Writings*, p.141.

19 Hawthorne's *Egotism, or The Bosom Serpent*, for example, tries to present 'real' snakes worming inside the breasts of sinners.

20 William Morris, *The Lindenborg Pool*, in *Early Romances in Prose and Verse* (London, 1973), pp.150–7.
21 Lytton, *A Strange Story* (Berkeley, 1973), p.170.
22 Lytton, *The Haunted and the Haunters* (1857), in *The Haunters and the Haunted*, ed. Ernest Rhys (London, 1921), p.99.
23 Oscar Wilde, *The Picture of Dorian Gray* (London, 1949), pp.104–5.
24 John Fowles, *The French Lieutenant's Woman* (London, 1970), p.319.
25 R.L. Stevenson, *The Strange Case of Dr Jekyll and Mr Hyde* (London, 1925), p.48 and p.51.
26 H.G. Wells, *The Island of Doctor Moreau* (London, 1946).
27 Bram Stoker, *Dracula*, p.181.
28 Paul Monette, *Nosferatu: The Vampyre* (London, 1970).
29 Freud, *Totem and Taboo* (London, 1950), p.142.
30 Richard Astle, 'Dracula as totemic monster: Lacan, Freud, Oedipus and history', see bibliography.
31 Bram Stoker, *The Lair of the White Worm* (London, 1960).

## 5 Fantastic realism

1 Terry Eagleton, *Criticism and Ideology*, p.161. Also Pierre Macherey, in *A Theory of Literary Production*, stresses the importance of reading a literary work in such a way as to discover its 'silences', all that has been excluded from it.
2 Charlotte Brontë, *Jane Eyre* (London, 1966); *Shirley* (London, 1974); *Villette* (London, 1949).
3 Showalter, *A Literature of their Own*, pp.114–25, discusses elements of 'madness' and fantasies of female freedom in *Jane Eyre*.
4 E.B. Browning, *Aurora Leigh*, introduced by Cora Kaplan (London, 1978). See the article 'Women's writing' cited in the bibliography.
5 Terry Eagleton's *Myths of Power* provides a Marxist analysis of these romance resolutions.
6 Elizabeth Gaskell, *Lois the Witch and Other Tales* (Leipzig,

1861); and *Mrs Gaskell's Tales of Mystery and Horror*, ed. Michael Ashley (London, 1978).

7  Mary Daly's *Gyn/Ecology: The Metaethics of Radical Feminism*, pp.178–222, discusses European witch-hunting as part of an obsessive desire to purify society of deviant and defiant women.

8  Emily Brontë, *Wuthering Heights* (London, 1965).

9  Balzac, *The Wild Ass's Skin*, tr. by H.J. Hunt (London, 1977), p.282.

10  Steven Marcus, 'Language into structure: *Pickwick Papers*', in *Representations*, pp.214–46.

11  Charles Dickens, *The New Oxford Illustrated Dickens*, 21 vols (Oxford, 1947–58).

12  A classic example of Dickens's use of the double is *A Tale of Two Cities*, where the 'hero' is divided between Charles Darnay (cultural self) and Sydney Carton (a 'careless' and 'reckless' other). There are numerous (literal) mirror images of their relationship. Darnay is to Carton his ideal ego. 'A good reason for taking to a man', says Carton, 'is that he shows you what you have fallen away from and what you might have been.' This other's (Carton's) illicit energies are sacrificed at the guillotine so that the self's 'better' version can live on, but Dickens implies the *waste* involved in this denial: as with Quilp's death, the murder of Carton brings the tale to a close.

13  Fyodor Dostoevsky, *Notes from Underground* and *The Double*, tr. by Jessie Coulson (London, 1972), p.23.

14  *The Gambler, Bobok, A Nasty Story*, tr. by Jessie Coulson (London, 1966), p.169.

15  F.R. Leavis, *The Great Tradition* (London, 1948).

16  George Eliot, *The Lifted Veil* (London, undated, first published in *Blackwood's Magazine*, 1859).

17  Henry James, *The Jolly Corner*, from *In the Cage and Other Tales* (London, 1958), pp.314–43.

18  Joseph Conrad, *The Secret Sharer*, in *Heart of Darkness and The Secret Sharer* (New York, 1969), p.138.

## 6   Victorian fantasies

1  See George Pitcher's article, 'Wittgenstein, nonsense and Lewis Carroll'.

2  See Phillips (ed.) *Aspects of Alice*, especially Paul Schilder's 'Psychoanalytic remarks on *Alice in Wonderland* and Lewis Carroll', pp.333–43.

3  Thomas Carlyle, *Sartor Resartus*, vol. 1, bk 3, p.210, in Carlyle's *Collected Works* (London, 1870).

4  George MacDonald, *Phantastes and Lilith* (London, 1962), pp.63–4.

5  Mary Daly, *Gyn/Ecology*, p.86, notes that Lilith corresponds to the Greek and Roman Lamia, and cites Raphael Patai's *The Hebrew Goddess*, which points to Lilith's revolutionary role: 'When Adam wished to lie with her, Lilith demurred: "Why should I lie beneath you", she asked, "when I am your equal since both of us were created from dust?" '

6  David Lodge, introduction to *Alton Locke* (London, 1967), p.xvii.

7  Maureen Duffy, *The Erotic World of Faery*, p.267, claims this desire as a longing for pre-natal uterine existence: 'Tom is at one and the same time the questing penis and the unborn foetus in its amniotic fluid.'

8  Charles Kingsley, *The Water Babies* (London, 1863), p.90.

9  Ursula Le Guin, *The City of Illusions* (London, 1971), p.152, for example: 'for there is in the long run no disharmony, only misunderstanding, no chance or mischance but only the ignorant eye.'

10 Randel Helms, *Myth, Magic and Meaning in Tolkien's World*, p.69: 'Tolkien's revulsion from the Orcs is a chief motive force behind *The Lord of the Rings*: they must be pushed back into Mordor and held there. Tolkien wants Orchood sealed in precisely the same underworld of the mind from which Blake wants it to erupt.'

## 7   From Kafka's 'Metamorphosis' to Pynchon's 'Entropy'

1  Julio Cortázar, *Blow-Up and Other Stories*, tr. by Paul Blackburn (New York, 1968), p.111.
2  Franz Kafka, *Metamorphosis*, tr. by Willa and Edwin Muir (London, 1961), p.28.
3  Mervyn Peake, *Titus Groan* (London, 1968), p.15.
4  Borges, *Tlon, Uqbar, Orbis Tertius*, in *Labyrinths* (London, 1970), pp.27–43: 'Tlon is surely a labyrinth, but it is a labyrinth devised by men, a labyrinth destined to be deciphered by men.' Its rigour is one 'of chess masters, not of angels' (p.42).
5  See Robert Scholes, *Fabulation and Metafiction* (1979).
6  Italo Calvino, *Invisible Cities*, tr. by William Weaver (London, 1979), pp.108–9.
7  Thomas Pynchon, *Entropy*, in Nelson Algren's *Book of Lonesome Monsters* (London, 1964), pp.169–85.
8  Pynchon, *Gravity's Rainbow* (London, 1975).
9  Pynchon, *The Crying of Lot 49* (New York, 1967), p.131.

## 8   Afterword: the 'unseen' of culture

1  Hélène Cixous, *Revue des sciences humaines*, December 1977, p.487.
2  Frieda Grafe and E. Patalas, *Suddeutsche Zeitung*, 9/10, February 1974, tr. by R. Mann, from Mark Nash, *Dreyer*, p.80.
3  Spenser, *The Faerie Queene*, Bk II, Canto 9, Stanza L.
4  Foucault, in his *Madness and Civilization*, draws analogies between 'madness' and 'fantastic' art. Modern 'fantasy' arraigns the world like madness does: 'by the madness which interrupts it, a work of art opens a void, a moment of silence, a question without answer, provokes a breach without reconciliation where the world is forced to question itself' (p.288).
5  Charles Nodier, 'The fantastic in literature', reprinted in Baronian's anthology, *La France fantastique de Balzac à Louys*, pp.17–31.

6 Geoffrey Harpham, 'The grotesque: first principles',
   *Journal of Aesthetics*, 34 (1975–6), 461–8.
7 Kafka, *Metamorphosis*, pp.27, 38.

# BIBLIOGRAPHY

THIS lists all secondary sources mentioned in the book, as well as indicating some other background reading. Works of literary fantasy are not included here: editions of texts are to be found in the notes.

The bibliography is split into three sections. The first (a) provides a fairly comprehensive catalogue of general works available on literary fantasy: readers wanting introductory criticism on the subject should refer to items marked *, whilst more incisive and theoretical studies are marked **. Remaining unmarked items are either general background, or in a foreign language. Psychoanalytic theory and criticism are listed separately in the second section (b), for the sake of easy reference, whilst the third section (c) deals with some critical works on individual authors. This last section does not aim to be exhaustive, but has selected works which are of especial interest in relation to some of the ideas introduced here. Although many of the items are, unfortunately, available only in French, they have been listed here, rather than excluded altogether, for English material is still very limited in its scope and method.

## (a) General and theoretical studies

ALTHUSSER, LOUIS, 'Ideology and ideological state apparatuses', in *Lenin and Philosophy and Other Essays* (London, 1971).

ARTAUD, ANTONIN, *The Theatre and its Double* (London, 1970).

AUERBACH, ERICH, *Mimesis* (Princeton, 1953).

** BAKHTIN, MIKHAIL, *Problems of Dostoevsky's Poetics*, tr. by R.W. Rotsel (Ardis, 1973).

* BARCLAY, GLEN ST JOHN, *Anatomy of Horror: The Masters of Occult Fiction* (London, 1978).

BARONIAN, JEAN BAPTISTE (ed.) *La France fantastique de Balzac à Louys: anthologie* (Verviers, 1973).

BARTHES, ROLAND, *Essais critiques* (Paris, 1964).

BATAILLE, GEORGES, *Literature and Evil*, tr. by Alastair Hamilton (London, 1973).

—— *Eroticism*, tr. by M. Dalwood (London, 1962).

—— *L'Impossible* (Paris, 1962).

BEAUVOIR, SIMONE DE, *Must we burn Sade?*, tr. by A. Michelson (London, 1953).

* BEER, GILLIAN, *The Romance* (London, 1970).

* —— 'Ghosts' [review article of Julia Briggs's *Night Visitors*], *Essays in Criticism*, 28 (July, 1978), 259–64.

BELLEMIN-NOÉL, JEAN, 'Des formes fantastiques aux thèmes fantasmatiques', *Littérature*, 2 (May, 1971), 103–28.

BELSEY, CATHERINE, *Critical Practice* (London, 1980).

BENNETT, TONY, *Formalism and Marxism* (London, 1979).

** BERSANI, LEO, *A Future for Astyanax: Character and Desire in Literature* (Toronto, 1976).

** BESSIÈRE, IRÈNE, *Le récit fantastique: la poétique de l'incertain* (Paris, 1974).

* BIRKHEAD, EDITH, *The Tale of Terror: A Study of the Gothic Romance* (London, 1921).

BLANCHOT, MAURICE, *L'espace littéraire* (Paris, 1955).

—— *Le livre à venir* (Paris, 1959).

—— *Le pas au-delà* (Paris, 1973).

BLEILER, EVERETT F., *The Checklist of Fantastic Literature* (Chicago, 1948).

BORGES, JORGE LOUIS, *Otrás Inquisiciones* (Buenos Aires, 1960).

\* BRIGGS, JULIA, *Night Visitors: The Rise and Fall of the English Ghost Story* (London, 1977).

BRION, MARCEL, *Art Fantastique* (Paris, 1961).

BUBER, MARTIN, *The Eclipse of God* (New York, 1952).

CAILLOIS, ROGER, *Au coeur du fantastique* (Paris, 1965).

—— *Images, Images: Essais sur le rôle et les pouvoirs de l'imagination* (Paris, 1966).

—— (ed.) *Anthologie du fantastique* (Paris, 1966).

CLARESON, THOMAS D. (ed.), *SF: The Other Side of Realism: Essays on Modern Fantasy and Science Fiction* (Ohio, 1971).

CLAYBOROUGH, ARTHUR, *The Grotesque in English Literature* (Oxford, 1965).

CLIFFORD, GAY, *The Transformations of Allegory* (London, 1974).

COLEMAN, WILLIAM EMMET, 'On the discrimination of gothicisms' (Unpublished Ph.D. dissertation, City University, New York, 1970).

COLERIDGE, SAMUEL TAYLOR, *Biographia Literaria*, first published 1817 (London, 1965).

COTT, JONATHAN (ed.) *Beyond the Looking Glass: Extraordinary Works of Fairy Tale and Fantasy* (New York, 1973).

CULLER, JONATHAN, *Structuralist Poetics* (London, 1975).

\* —— 'Literary fantasy', in 'Fantasy in Literature' issue of *Cambridge Review*, 95 (1973), 30–3.

DALY, MARY, *Gyn/Ecology: The Metaethics of Radical Feminism* (London, 1979).

DÉDÉYAN, CHARLES, *Le thème de Faust dans la littérature européenne*, 5 vols. (Paris, 1954–67).

DERRIDA, JACQUES, *L'écriture et la différence* (Paris, 1967).

DUFFY, MAUREEN, *The Erotic World of Faery* (London, 1974).

EAGLETON, TERRY, *Marxism and Literary Criticism* (London, 1976).

—— *Criticism and Ideology: A Study in Marxist Literary Theory* (London, 1976).

ELIADE, MIRCEA, *The Two and the One* (Méphistophélès et l'androgyne), tr. by J.M. Cohen (London, 1965).

* 'Faery, fantasy and pseudo-medievalia in twentieth-century literature', *Mosaic*, 10, no. 2 (Winter, 1977).

FIEDLER, LESLIE A., *Love and Death in the American Novel* (New York, 1960).

FLETCHER, ANGUS, *Allegory: The Theory of a Symbolic Mode* (Cornell, 1964).

FOUCAULT, MICHEL, *Madness and Civilization: A History of Insanity in the Age of Reason*, tr. by R. Howard (London, 1967).

—— 'Préface à la transgression', *Critique*, 195–6 (1963), 751–69.

—— *The Order of Things: An Archaeology of the Human Sciences* (London, 1970).

FRANKL, PAUL, *The Gothic: Literary Sources and Interpretations through Eight Centuries* (Princeton, 1960).

FRANZ, M.L. VON, *Problems of the Feminine in Fairy Tales* (New York, 1974).

FRYE, NORTHROP, 'The mythos of summer: romance', in *Anatomy of Criticism: Four Essays* (Princeton, 1957).

—— *The Secular Scripture: A Study of the Structure of Romance* (Harvard, 1976).

GILLMAN, LINDA, 'The problem of language in Leiris, Bataille and Blanchot' (Unpublished Ph.D dissertation, University of Cambridge, 1980).

GIRARD, RENÉ NOËL, *Deceit, Desire, and the Novel: Self and Other in Literary Structure*, tr. by Y. Freccero (Baltimore, 1965).

—— *Violence and the Sacred*, tr. by P. Gregory (Baltimore, 1977).

GOETHE, JOHANN WOLFGANG VON, *Truth and Fiction Relating to My Life (1811–1822)*, tr. by J. Oxenford (Boston, 1822).

GUIOMAR, MICHEL, 'L'insolite', *Revue d'Esthétique*, 10

(1957), 113–44.

—— 'Pour une poétique de la peur', *Problèmes*, 74–5 (1961), 90–104.

HARPHAM, GEOFFREY, 'The grotesque: first principles', *Journal of Aesthetics*, 34 (1975–6), 461–8.

HART, FRANCIS RUSSELL, 'The experiene of character in the English gothic novel', in *Experience in the Novel: Selected Papers from the English Institute*, ed. Roy Harvey Pearce (New York, 1968), 83–105.

HARTMANN, GEOFFREY, 'The fullness and nothingness of literature', *Yale French Studies*, 16 (Winter, 1955–6), 63–78.

HARVEY, W.J., *Character and the Novel* (London, 1965).

HASSAN, IHAB, *The Dismemberment of Orpheus* (New York, 1971).

HAWKES, TERENCE, *Structuralism and Semiotics* (London, 1977).

HEBDIGE, DICK, *Subculture: The Meaning of Style* (London, 1979).

HEGEL, G.W.F., *The Phenomenology of Mind* (1807), tr. by J.B. Baillie (London, 1931).

HELLENS, FRANZ, *Le fantastique réel* (Paris, 1967).

HOCKE, G.R., *Labyrinthe de l'art fantastique* (Paris, 1967).

HUME, ROBERT D., 'Gothic versus romantic: a revaluation of the gothic novel', *PMLA*, 84 (1969), 282–90.

*   IRWIN, WILLIAM R., *The Game of the Impossible: A Rhetoric of Fantasy* (Illinois, 1976).

JACKSON, ROSEMARY, 'Dickens and the gothic tradition' (Unpublished D. Phil dissertation, University of York, 1978).

—— 'The Silenced Text: Shades of Gothic in Victorian Fiction', *Minnesota Review*, 13 (Fall, 1979), 98–112.

**   JAMESON, FREDRIC, 'Magical narratives: romance as genre', *New Literary History*, 7, no. 1 (Autumn, 1975), 133–63.

—— *Marxism and Form* (Princeton, 1971).

—— *The Prison-House of Language: A Critical Account of Struc-*

*turalism and Russian Formalism* (Princeton, 1972).

JOSIPOVICI, GABRIEL, *The World and the Book* (London, 1973).

\* KAYSER, WOLFGANG, *The Grotesque in Art and Literature*, tr. by U. Weisstein (Indiana, 1963).

KENNARD, JEAN E., *Number and Nightmare: Forms of Fantasy in Contemporary Fiction* (Hamden, Conn., 1975).

\* KIELY, ROBERT, *The Romantic Novel in England* (Harvard, 1972).

KNIGHT, EVERETT, *A Theory of the Classical Novel* (London, 1970).

KRISTEVA, JULIA, 'Une poétique ruinée', Introductory essay to French edition of Bakhtin's *La poétique de Dostoevsky* (Paris, 1970).

—— *La révolution du langage poétique* (Paris, 1976).

LEAVIS, F.R., *The Great Tradition* (London, 1948).

LESSER, SIMON, *Fiction and the Unconscious* (London, 1960).

LÉVY, MAURICE, *Le roman gothique anglais 1764–1824* (Toulouse, 1968).

LEWIS, C.S., *Of Other Worlds*, ed. W. Hooper (London, 1966).

\* LOVECRAFT, HOWARD P., *Supernatural Horror in Literature*, introduced by E.F. Bleiler (New York, 1973).

LUKÁCS, GEORG, *The Meaning of Contemporary Realism*, tr. by John and Necke Mander (London, 1963).

LÜTHI, MAX, *Once Upon a Time: On the Nature of Fairy Tales* (New York, 1970).

MABILLE, PIERRE, *Le miroir du merveilleux* (Paris, 1962).

MACDONALD, GEORGE, 'The fantastic imagination', published in *A Dish of Orts, Chiefly Papers on the Imagination, and on Shakespeare* (London, 1893).

MACHEREY, PIERRE, *A Theory of Literary Production,* tr. by Geoffrey Wall (London, 1978).

MACNIECE, LOUIS, *Varieties of Parable* (Cambridge, 1965).

MCNUTT, DAN J., *The Eighteenth Century Gothic Novel: An Annotated Bibliography of Criticism and Selected Texts* (New York and London, 1975).

MALIN, IRVING, *New American Gothic* (Carbondale, 1962).

* MANLOVE, C.N., *Modern Fantasy: Five Studies* (Cambridge, 1975).

MARCUS, STEVEN, *Representations: Essays on Literature and Society* (New York, 1975).

MARX, KARL and ENGELS, FRIEDRICH, *The German Ideology* (London, 1974).

—— *Selected Works* (London, 1968).

** MASSEY, IRVING, *The Gaping Pig: Literature and Metamorphosis* (California, 1976).

MATTHEWS, J.H., *Surrealism and the Novel* (Michigan, 1966).

MILNER, MAX, *Le diable dans la littérature française de Cazotte à Baudelaire 1772–1861*, 2 vols (Paris, 1960).

MIYOSHI, MASAO, *The Divided Self: A Perspective on the Literature of the Victorians* (New York, 1969).

MOERS, ELLEN, *Literary Women* (London, 1977).

** NASH, MARK, '*Vampyr* and the fantastic', *Screen*, 17, no. 3 (Autumn, 1976), 29–67.

—— *Dreyer* (London, 1977).

NELSON, COWRY, JR., 'Night thoughts on the gothic novel', *Yale Review*, 52 (1962), 236–57.

NODIER, CHARLES, 'Du fantastique en littérature', published by *Revue de Paris*, 1830. Reprinted by Baronian (see above), 17–31.

OWSTROWSKI, WITOLD, 'The fantastic and the realistic in literature: suggestions on how to define and analyse fantastic fiction', *Zagadnienia Rodzajow Literackich*, 9 (1966), 54–71.

PARSONS, COLEMAN O., *Witchcraft and Demonology in Scott's Fiction: With Chapters on the Supernatural in Scottish Literature* (Edinburgh, 1964).

* PENZOLDT, PETER, *The Supernatural in Fiction* (London, 1952).

PIAGET, JEAN, *Judgement and Reasoning in the Child* (London, 1928).

PLATO, *The Republic*, tr. by Desmond Lee (London, 1955).

* PRAWER, SIEGBERT S., *The 'Uncanny' in Literature: An Apol-*

*ogy for its Investigation* (London, 1965).

PRAZ, MARIO, *The Romantic Agony*, tr. by A. Davidson (London, 1970).

PRÉDAL, RENÉ, *Le cinéma fantastique* (Paris, 1970).

\* PRICKETT, STEPHEN, *Victorian Fantasy* (Sussex, 1979).

PROPP, VLADIMIR, *The Morphology of the Folk-Tale*, tr. by Lawrence Scott, 2nd edn (Texas, 1968).

\* PUNTER, DAVID, *The Literature of Terror* (London, 1980).

\* RABKIN, ERIC S., *The Fantastic in Literature* (Princeton, 1976).

*Ranam (Recherches Anglaises et Americaines)*, 6 (1973), edition 'Le fantastique'.

REEVE, CLARA, *The Progress of Romance* (1785), ed. E.M. McGill (New York, 1930).

RETINGER, JOSEPH H., *Le conte fantastique dans le romantisme français*, first published Paris 1909 (Geneva, 1973).

RUDWIN, M.J., *The Devil in Legend and Literature* (Chicago, 1931).

RUSS, JOANNA, 'The subjunctivity of science fiction', *Extrapolation*, 15, part 1, 51–9.

SADE, MARQUIS DE, *Reflections on the Novel* (1800), in *The 120 Days of Sodom and Other Writings* (New York, 1966).

\*\* SARTRE, JEAN PAUL, ' "Aminadab" or the fantastic considered as a language', in *Situations*, I (Paris, 1947), 56–72.

\* SCARBOROUGH, DOROTHY, *The Supernatural in Modern English Fiction* (New York, 1917).

SCHLEGEL, FRIEDRICH, *The Philosophy of Life and the Philosophy of Language* (London, 1847).

SCHNEIDER, MARCEL, *La littérature fantastique en France* (Paris, 1964).

SCHOLES, ROBERT and KELLOGG, ROBERT L., *The Nature of Narrative* (New York, 1966).

SCHOLES, ROBERT, *Structural Fabulation* (Indiana, 1975).

—— *Fabulation and Metafiction* (Illinois, 1979).

SCHUHL, PIERRE-MAXIME, *Le merveilleux, la pensée et l'action* (Paris, 1952).

\* SEWELL, ELIZABETH, *The Field of Nonsense* (London, 1952).

SHOWALTER, ELAINE, *A Literature of Their Own: British Women Novelists from Brontë to Lessing* (Princeton, 1977).

SMEED, J.W., *Faust in Literature* (Oxford, 1975).

SOLLERS, PHILIPPE, *L'écriture et l'experience des limites* (Paris, 1968).

SORIANO, MARC, *Les contes de Perrault: culture savante et traditions populaires* (Paris, 1968).

STERN, J.P., *On Realism* (London, 1973).

SUMMERS, MONTAGUE, *A Gothic Bibliography* (London, 1941).

\* —— *The Gothic Quest: A History of the Gothic Novel* (London, 1938).

SUVIN, DARKO, *Metamorphosis of Science Fiction: On the Poetics and History of a Literary Genre* (Yale, 1979).

SYMONDS, JOHN ADDINGTON, 'Caricature, the fantastic, the grotesque', in *Essays Speculative and Suggestive*, 2 vols. (London, 1980), I, 240–55.

THALMANN, MARIANNE, *The Romantic Fairy Tale: The Seeds of Surrealism* (Michigan, 1964).

\*\* THOMPSON, GARY R. (ed.), *'The Gothic Imagination: Essays in Dark Romanticism* (Washington, 1974).

\*\* TODOROV, TZVETAN, *The Fantastic: A Structural Approach to a Literary Genre*, tr. by Richard Howard (London, 1973).

—— 'The fantastic in fiction', tr. by Vivienne Mylne, *Twentieth Century Studies*, 3 (1970), 76–92.

\* TOLKIEN, J.R.R., 'On fairy stories', in *Tree and Leaf* (London, 1964).

\* VARMA, DEVENDRA P., *The Gothic Flame: Being a History of the Gothic Novel in England: its Origins, Efflorescence, Disintegration, and Residuary Influences* (London, 1957).

VAX, LOUIS, 'L'art de faire peur', *Critique*, I (November, 1957), 915–42; II (December, 1957), 1026–48.

—— 'Le fantastique, la raison, et l'art', *Revue philosophique de la France et de l'étranger*, 86 (1961), 319–48.

—— *La séduction de l'étrange: étude sur la littérature fantastique* (Paris, 1965).

—— *L'art et la littérature fantastiques* (Paris, 1974).

WAIN, MARIANNE, 'The double in romantic narrative: a preliminary study', *Germanic Review*, 36 (1961), 257–68.

WATT, IAN, *The Rise of the Novel* (London, 1957).

WOLFF, ROBERT LEE, *Strange Stories, and Other Explorations in Victorian Fiction* (Boston, Mass., 1971).

*Working Paper in Cultural Studies*, 10, 'On ideology' (Birmingham, 1977).

\* ZIOLKOWSKI, THEODORE, *Disenchanted Images: A Literary Iconology* (Princeton, 1977).

### (b) Psychoanalytic theory

ADLAM, DIANA et al., 'Psychology, ideology and the human subject', *Ideology and Consciousness*, 1 (May, 1977), 5–56.

BOWIE, MALCOLM, 'Jacques Lacan', in *Structuralism and Since*, ed. John Sturrock (Oxford, 1979).

BROWN, NORMAN O., *Life Against Death: The Psychoanalytical Meaning of History* (London, 1968).

CIXOUS, HÉLÈNE, 'La fiction et ses fantômes: une lecture de l'*Unheimliche* de Freud', *Poétique*, 10 (1973), 199–216.

—— 'The character of "character" ', tr. by Keith Cohen, *New Literary History*, 5, ii (Winter, 1974), 383–402.

—— *Les prénoms de personne* (Paris, 1974).

ELLENBERGER, H.F., *The Discovery of the Unconscious* (New York, 1970).

FREUD, SIGMUND, *The Standard Edition of the Complete Psychological Works*, tr. and ed. by James Strachey, 24 vols. (London, 1953).

—— Essay on 'The uncanny', vol. 17, 217–52.

—— *Introductory Lectures on Psychoanalysis* (London, 1973).

HEUSCHER, JULIUS E., *A Psychiatric Study of Myths and Fairy Tales: Their Origin, Meaning and Usefulness* (Springfield, 1974).

HUNTER, RICHARD and MACALPINE, IDA, *Three Hundred Years of Psychiatry 1535–1860* (London, 1963).

IRIGARAY, LUCE, 'Women's exile', *Ideology and Consciousness*, 1 (May, 1977) 62–76.

JAMESON, FREDRIC, 'Imaginary and symbolic in Lacan: Marxism, psychoanalytic criticism, and the problem of the subject', *Yale French Studies*, 55/56 (1977), 338–95.

KAPLAN, CORA, 'Language and gender', *Papers on Patriarchy* (Brighton, 1976), 21–37.

KEPPLER, C.F., *The Literature of the Second Self* (Tuscan, 1972).

LACAN, JACQUES, *The Language of the Self: The Function of Language in Psychoanalysis*, introduced by Anthony Wilden (Baltimore and London, 1968).

—— *Ecrits: A Selection*, tr. by Alan Sheridan (London, 1977).

—— *The Four Fundamental Concepts of Psychoanalysis*, tr. by Alan Sheridan (London, 1977).

LAPLANCHE, J. and PONTALIS, J–B., *The Language of Psychoanalysis*, tr. by Donald Nicholson-Smith (London, 1973).

MARCUSE, HERBERT, *Eros and Civilisation: A Philosophical Inquiry into Freud* (London, 1969).

MITCHELL, JULIET, *Psychoanalysis and Feminism* (London, 1974).

RANK, OTTO, *The Double: A Psychoanalytic Study*, tr. and ed. by H. Tucker, Jr. (N. Carolina, 1971).

REID, THOMAS, *Essays on the Intellectual Powers of Man* (1785), ed. A.D. Woozley (London, 1941).

—— *An Inquiry into the Human Mind, On the Principles of Common Sense* (1764), ed. T. Duggan (Chicago, 1970).

RICHARDSON, MAURICE, 'The psychoanalysis of ghost stories', *Twentieth Century*, 166 (1959), 419–31.

ROGERS, ROBERT, *A Psychoanalytic Study of the Double in Literature* (Detroit, 1970).

RUITENBEEK, HENDRIK M. (ed.), *Psychoanalysis and Literature* (New York, 1964).

SARTRE, JEAN PAUL, *Imagination: A Psychological Critique*, tr. by F. Williams (Ann Arbor, 1962).

TYMMS, RALPH VINCENT, *Doubles in Literary Psychology* (Cambridge, 1949).

WEEDON, C. and BURNISTON, S., 'Ideology, subjectivity

and the artistic text', in *On Ideology*, Centre for Contemporary Cultural Studies (London, 1978).

WHITE, ALLON H., 'L'éclatement du sujet: the theoretical work of Julia Kristeva', *Centre for Contemporary Cultural Studies Working Paper* (Birmingham, 1977).

## (c)   Studies of individual authors

ARNAUD, ALAIN, *Bataille* (Paris, 1978).

ASTLE, RICHARD, 'Dracula as totemic monster: Lacan, Freud, Oedipus and history', *Sub-stance*, 25 (1980), 98–105.

BACHELARD, GASTON, *Lautréamont* (Paris, 1939).

BARTHES, ROLAND, *Sade, Fourier, Loyola* (Paris, 1971).

BATCHELOR, JOHN, *Mervyn Peake: A Biographical and Critical Exploration* (London, 1974).

BLANCHOT, MAURICE, *Lautréamont et Sade* (Paris, 1963).

BONAPARTE, MARIE, *The Life and Works of Edgar Allan Poe: A Psychoanalytic Interpretation*, tr. by John Rodker (London, 1949).

BROOKE-ROSE, CHRISTINE, 'The squirm of the true,' *Poetics and Theory of Literature*, I (1976), 265–94 and 513–46; II (1977), 517–62.

BURKHART, CHARLES, *Charlotte Brontë: A Psychosexual Study of her Novels* (London, 1973).

CAREY, JOHN, *The Violent Effigy: A Study of Dickens' Imagination* (London, 1973).

CHITTY, SUSAN, *The Beast and the Monk: A Life of Charles Kingsley* (London, 1974).

DAVIS, EARLE R., *The Flint and the Flame: The Artistry of Charles Dickens* (London, 1964).

EAGLETON, TERRY, *Myths of Power: A Marxist Study of the Brontës* (London, 1975).

EMPSON, WILLIAM, 'Alice in Wonderland: the child as swain', in *Some Versions of Pastoral* (London, 1966).

FANGER, DONALD, *Dostoevsky's Romantic Realism: A Study of*

*Dostoevsky in Relation to Balzac, Dickens, and Gogol* (Harvard, 1965).

GATTEGNO, JEAN, 'Folie, croyance et fantastique dans *Dracula*', *Littérature*, 8 (1972), 72–83.

GIFFORD, DOUGLAS, *James Hogg* (Edinburgh, 1976).

GIRARD, RENÉ NOÉL *Dostoïevski, du double à l'unité* (Paris, 1963).

GOLDBERG, M.A., 'Moral and myth in Mrs Shelley's *Frankenstein*', *Keats-Shelley Journal*, 8 (1959), 27–38.

HELMS, RANDEL, *Myth, Magic and Meaning in Tolkien's World* (London, 1974).

HILLEGAS, MARK R. (ed.), *The Shadows of Imagination: The Fantasies of C.S. Lewis, J.R.R. Tolkien, and Charles Williams* (S. Illinois, 1969).

IDMAN, NIILO, *Charles Robert Maturin: His Life and Works* (London, 1923).

KETTERER, DAVID, *Frankenstein's Creation: The Book, The Monster and Human Reality* (Wellington, Univ. of Victoria, 1979).

KLOSSOWSKI, PIERRE, *Sade et Fourier* (Paris, 1974).

LARY, N.M., *Dostoevsky and Dickens: A Study of Literary Influence* (London, 1973).

LEVINE, GEORGE and LEVERENZ, DAVID (eds.), *Mindful Pleasures: Essays on Thomas Pynchon* (Boston and Toronto, 1976).

LEVINE, GEORGE and KNOEPFLMACHER, V.C. (eds.), *The Endurance of Frankenstein: Essays on Mary Shelley's Novel* (California, 1979).

LINNÉR, SVEN, *Dostoevsky on Realism* (Stockholm, 1967).

LYLES, W.H., *Mary Shelley: An Annotated Bibliography* (New York, 1975).

MOGLEN, HÉLÈNE, *Charlotte Brontë: The Self Conceived* (New York, 1976).

NORMAND, JEAN, *Nathaniel Hawthorne* (London, 1970).

PHILLIPS, ROBERT (ed.), *Aspects of Alice* (London, 1971).

PHILLIPS, WALTER C., *Dickens, Reade and Collins: Sensation Novelists* (New York, 1919).

PITCHER, GEORGE, 'Wittgenstein, nonsense and Lewis Carroll', *Massachusetts Review*, 6, no.3 (Spring/Summer, 1965), 591–611.

PRENDERGAST, CHRISTOPHER, *Balzac: Fiction and Melodrama* (London, 1978).

ROBERT, MARTHE, *Kafka* (Paris, 1960).

—— 'L'inconscient, creuset de l'oeuvre', *Dostoïevski* (Paris, 1971).

SIEGEL, MARK RICHARD, *Pynchon: Creative Paranoia in Gravity's Rainbow* (New York and London, 1978).

SIMPSON, LOUIS, *James Hogg: A Critical Study* (London, 1962).

SMALL, CHRISTOPHER, *Mary Shelley's Frankenstein: Tracing the Myth* (Pittsburgh, 1973).

SPARK, MURIEL, *Child of Light: A Reassessment of Mary Wollstonecraft Shelley* (Essex, 1951).

SPILKA, MARK, *Dickens and Kafka: A Mutual Interpretation* (Indiana, 1963).

STOEHR, TAYLOR, *Dickens: The Dreamer's Stance* (New York, 1965).

*Tel Quel*, 28 (Winter, 1967), volume on 'La pensée de Sade'.

TODOROV, TZVETAN, 'The ghosts of Henry James', in *The Poetics of Prose*, tr. by Richard Howard (New York, 1977).

WASIOLEK, EDWARD, *Dostoevsky: The Major Fiction* (Cambridge, Mass., 1964).

WELSH, ALEXANDER, *The City of Dickens* (Oxford, 1971).

'Women's writing: Jane Eyre, Shirley, Villette, Aurora Leigh', The Marxist-Feminist Literature Collective, *Ideology and Consciousness*, 3 (Spring, 1978), 27–48.

WOOLF, ROBERT LEE, *The Golden Key: A Study of the Fiction of George MacDonald* (New Haven, 1961).

# NAME INDEX

# SUBJECT INDEX